Ngugi's Novels and African History

Ngugi's Novels and African History

Narrating the Nation

James Ogude

Pluto Press

LONDON • STERLING, VIRGINIA

First published 1999 by Pluto Press
345 Archway Road, London N6 5AA
and 22883 Quicksilver Drive,
Sterling, VA 21066–2012, USA

British Library Cataloguing in Publication Data
A catalogue record for this book is available from
the British Library

ISBN 0 7453 1436 8 hbk

Library of Congress Cataloging in Publication Data
Ogude, James.
    Ngugi's novels and African history: narrating the nation / James
    Ogude
        p.   cm.
    ISBN 0–7453–1436–8 hbk
    1. Ngũgĩ wa Thiong'o, 1938–   —Knowledge—History. 2. Historical
fiction, Kenyan (English)—History and criticism. 3. Literature and
history—African—History—20th century. 4. Literature and history–
–Kenya—History—20th century. 5. Ngũgĩ wa Thiong'o. 1938–
–Fictional works. I. Title.
PR9381.9.N45Z82   1999
823—dc21   99–23065
                                                                  CIP

Designed and produced for Pluto Press by
Chase Production Services, Chadlington, OX7 3LN
Typeset from disk by Stanford DTP Services, Northampton
Printed in the EC by TJ International, Padstow

Contents

To my brother Aguyo Kogude, who sacrificed for my education and to my mother Helida Akuno Ogude for showing me the value of discipline and hard work.

Acknowledgements

Ngugi's stature in African literature and his interventions in the debates on Africa's historiography have been major influences on my academic career. My first encounter with the social relevance of literature was through my contact with Ngugi as a student at Nairobi University and I thank him for the insights without which this book would have been different. Special gratitude goes to my academic mentor, Njabulo Ndebele, and to members of the African Literature Department at the University of the Witwatersrand, especially Phaswane Mpe, Isabel Hofmeyr and Bheki Peterson for their support and encouragement. Mpe in particular helped with the initial proofreading of the manuscript – many thanks. Special thanks to the African literature students, whose stimulating debates in class helped to sharpen some of the ideas expressed in this book. And to my friend, Atieno Odhiambo of Rice University, Texas, for his support and useful sources on the production of Kenyan history.

Although this book is based on my PhD thesis written for the University of the Witwatersrand, South Africa, it has been revised substantially to include the early novels of Ngugi and to provide a more comprehensive historical perspective – thanks to Roger van Zwanenberg of Pluto Press for insisting that I include the early novels of Ngugi. I have also endeavoured to simplify the academic jargon and terminology originally used in the thesis in order to make the book accessible to a wider audience without compromising the academic value the book may have. Some parts of this book have appeared as articles in various journals. Parts of the introduction and Chapter 1 were drawn from 'Ngugi's Concept of History' in the *Canadian Journal of African Studies* 31.1. (1997): 86–112. Parts of Chapter 4 appeared in English in *Africa* 24.1 (1997): 71–87 and parts of Chapter 6 were drawn from my article appearing in *Wasafiri* 28 (Autumn 1988): 3–9. Where permission has been required for republication, I am grateful to the editors of the journals for that permission.

Finally, I would like to thank members of my family who have sustained me with encouragement throughout this project: to my daughter, Didi, my son, Omondi, and to my wife, Nthabiseng, for love and understanding as I kept away from their company while preparing this book.

Introduction

Writing Back and the Restoration of a Community/Nation

Early African narratives have always been seen as writing against colonial discursive practices in an attempt to validate Africa's historiography denied by colonialism. Chinua Achebe, the Nigerian writer, called it 'an act of atonement' (quoted in Awonoor 1976, p. 251) – the process of returning to self or what Basil Davidson calls the reconstituting of a 'shattered community, to save or restore the sense and fact of community against all the pressures of the colonial system' (1978, p. 155). Edward Said calls it restoring 'the imprisoned community to itself' (1994, p. 259). In literature, this process of restoration was marked by a strong sense of cultural nationalism.

The emergence of cultural nationalism as an engagement with the epistemological practices that came with colonialism was an attempt at the recovery of African gnosis repressed by colonialism. These forms of African writings, rooted in the emergent African nationalism, were engaged in what Gikandi calls 'the act of willing new realities into being' and elaborating new knowledges of Africa (1991, p. 2). Significantly, the knowledges were reconstructed not simply from what colonialism was attempting to repress, but also from the historical conditions colonialism had created. The nationalist thought depended, in part, upon the realities of the colonial powers and the discursive practices that came with it. But the new narrative of 'nation formation' constituted a dialogue, not just with the West whose discursive instruments the writers had appropriated to subvert the colonial project, but also a dialogue with other adjacent zones of knowledge such as history, anthropology, political science, religion, etc., within the academy. In other words, the process of social engineering, the process of specifying the

1

ideological lexicon of nation formation, involved the African writer as much as it involved the historian, the political scientist, the anthropologist, the politician and the religious leader. The sites of construction and idioms may have been different, but they certainly interfaced and interlocked in search of an enduring moral centre.

Ngugi has been most poignant in his engagement with other disciplines and the discursive practices emanating from the West. Narrative, particularly the novel, has tended to provide Ngugi with the space to imagine Africa's history which he believes had been repressed by colonialism. Ngugi has insisted, correctly, that his writing is very much part of Kenya's (and by implication Africa's) historiography and the theorising of its political economy. Ngugi's writing is not just laying a claim to the terrain of culture, but also to radically 'revised visions of the past tending towards a postcolonial future, as urgently reinterpretable and redeployable experiences, in which the formerly silent native speaks and acts on territory reclaimed as part of a general movement of resistance, from the colonist' (Said 1994, p. 256). Ngugi posits narrative here as an agent of history because it provides the space for challenging our notions of national identities, uses of history, and ways in which they are deployed in power contestation in modern Kenya and Africa in general.

And yet, in spite of Ngugi's interest in the grand project of writing back to colonialist historiography, and in spite of the apparent radical reinterpretations that have been hailed in his novels ranging from *The River Between* (1965) to *Matigari* (1987), the element of historical invention has not been adequately explored. The element of historical invention could provide a useful point of entry into Ngugi's concept of history, particularly when one bears in mind Ngugi's stated commitment to presenting 'true' images of Africa's past as a counter to 'false' colonial portrayals of the continent (Ngugi 1972, pp. 39–46).

This book seeks to look beyond the current state of criticism which has failed to locate Ngugi's texts within the contested terrain of Kenya's historiography.[1] Critics have been content to take their image of Africa from the literature itself and then praise the literature for its 'truth' or lack of it without trying to understand the nuances underpinning the alternative histories embedded in these texts. If Ngugi sets out to offer an alternative picture – 'the true image of Africa' – then we need to enquire into the 'truth' of his picture in order to avoid the temptation to erase the problematics and contradictory meanings of his texts.

The need to rethink Ngugi's texts in the light of new experiences and theoretical insights is desirable if we want to enrich the production of knowledges in Africa. The call for rereading Ngugi's texts does not imply that the 'first' readings were entirely useless or even irrelevant. In this book I anticipate the kind of interrogation that would bring to the surface certain things that may have been taken for granted due to a number of factors, for example, the trend closely associated with the 'new criticism' which tends to isolate the text from its social and historical setting. A literary text at its best, we are told, should express some timelessness, which could be demonstrated even if one ignores time and specificity. But of particular interest to me is the now well rehashed debate around the literature/history couplet in which literature is seen as the signifier and history the signified. This approach, which privileges history as the source of literature, tends to overemphasise literature's fictiveness and to delete its historical and political relevance. The fundamentals of this argument are that literature and history belong to different spheres of being in which history is regarded as more basic and '"more real" ... than the domain of textual representations' (Bennet 1990, p. 42). The effect of this dualistic ontology, Tony Bennet writes, 'is to privilege history as both the literature's source and its ultimate referent' (p. 42). In other words, 'literature always constitutes the phenomenon to be explained just as surely as history provides the means of explanation; no other ordering of their relations is imaginable' (p. 42). Ultimately, the explanatory power or even the epistemological usefulness of literature depends on how close it approximates the historical truth which is its ultimate referent. Thus 'the political effects and value of literary texts are assessed on the basis of the position accorded them in relation to the independently known history' (p. 42) which is assigned the status of their ultimate referent.

I take the view that fiction is a representation of history. And to the extent that both history and fiction deploy narrative structure, Mink writes, they can both be seen as 'a primary and irreducible form of human comprehension, an article in the constitution of common sense' (1978, p. 132). For this reason, narrative has increasingly come to be regarded as a type of explanation and a form of knowledge as forceful as so-called 'scientific knowledge' (White 1987, p. xi; Mink 1978, p. 133). White makes much the same point when he argues that the historical text is necessarily a literary artefact because the process of creative imagination involves the writer of fiction as much as it does the historian.[2]

The point is that both fiction and history, while having marked differences, also share vast similarities. Both history and literature invoke the principle of selection and derive their material from specific cultures and historical experiences. According to Tony Bennet, 'History does not supply a key with which to unlock the meaning of the literary text, nor does the latter function merely as a particular route into the study of a history conceived as a set of realities outside its own boundaries' (1990, p. 71), but rather, the literary text should be seen as part of the wider historiography in its own right. Most critics desist from treating Ngugi's texts as part of Kenya's historiography. I am hoping that this book will reassert Ngugi's narrative within the contested terrain of Kenya's historiography.

What, then, is the substance of Ngugi's historical invention? Has it remained consistent throughout his works? How does Ngugi's idea of history influence the choices of narrative strategies he makes in his novels? These are some of the issues I seek to explore in this introduction and the chapters that follow. A closer look at Ngugi's works will reveal that they are contingent, in many ways, on the sociopolitical climate of Kenya at the time of their creation. Ian Glenn has made this point in an interesting if problematic article[3] which attempts to relate the deep structures of Ngugi's novels to the ambiguous position of the 'elite' in independent Africa. However, this point notwithstanding, I would suggest that to have a nuanced understanding of Ngugi's texts one has to grapple more closely with the intellectual climate – the pertinent issues and debates – within which his novels were located at the time of their writing.

Nationalism, Ethnicity and Individualism

In Ngugi's earlier texts one is forced to grapple with the notion of nationalism and other related issues such as ethnicity and individualism that confronted the African writers in their attempt to define the new nation-state and, more importantly, to give an alternative African historiography. The bedrock of this new African historiography was nationalism: what Frederick Cooper has described as an attempt to 'put together "Africa" in the face of general perceptions of everlasting and immutable divisions' (1994, p. 1519), or what Edward Said defines as 'an assertion of belonging in and to a place, a people, a heritage. It affirms the home created by a community of language, culture and customs; and, by so doing, it fends off exile, fights to prevent its ravages' (1984, p. 162).

If we accept for a moment that Ngugi's earlier texts are linked to the problematic of the nationalist discourse of the early 1960s and beyond, then we need to interrogate the notion of nationalism by drawing on the work of certain theorists who have reconceptualised nationalism.[4] The major point of this reconceptualisation has been to stress the inventive nature of nationalist ideologies rather than the organic, 'natural' explanations which nationalism traditionally gives to itself. This process of invention is of course highly contradictory and I will attempt to argue that Ngugi's earlier texts were written in just such an ambiguous moment of national invention and that the texts bear the imprints of these contradictions.

Manufacturing Nationalism and the East African Experience

Recent scholarship has pointed to the close link that exists between the notion of the nation and the book. Benedict

Anderson, for example, has focused on the development of print language as a primary terrain in which the idea of the nation is constituted: 'these forms (the novel and the newspaper) provided the technical means for "re-presenting" the kind of imagined community that is the nation' (1983, p. 30). The idea of the nation, as Anderson stresses, emerged when print capitalism provided a medium to establish a bounded identity. As early as 1972, Ali Mazrui made a similar point in *Cultural Engineering and Nation Building in East Africa* when he drew attention to the close link between cultural engineering and the printed word. Mazrui was both validating and reinforcing literature's role in nationalism. Mazrui was by no means a lone voice on this issue in East Africa because many others entered the debate on how to manufacture a suitably nationalistic literature for East African countries. Taban lo Liyong, for example, talked of a 'literary barrenness' in East Africa and argued that a nation without writers is a dying nation (1969, pp. 23–42).

Whether we agree with lo Liyong's infamous statement is beside the point. The point is that certain people felt there was a lack of appropriate literature that could give some substance to the idea of East African nations. Ngugi – studying in Makerere, editor of *Penpoint*, author of several short stories and working in drama – was no doubt centrally involved in these debates. Much of his thinking was coloured by an orthodox nationalism and he saw the writer as having a socially prominent role in the formation of the nation. Writers, he said, 'are the herald of a new awareness of the emergent Africa' (quoted in Lindfors 1981, p. 30). However, his nationalist orientation, like that of others, was shot through with contradictions. On the most obvious level elements of his Christianity and liberal individualism cut across his sentiments on nationalism and the writer's role within it (Ngugi 1972, p. 32). At a subtle level, Ngugi, like many nationalists in the colonies, was also caught up in the colonial definitions of nationalism. He was implicated in what was 'a derivative discourse': the nation-centred nationalism rooted in the kind of modernist politics that eventually had a major influence on the colonies, focusing on the European-defined boundaries and institutions, and on notions of progress shaped by capitalism and European social thought. But he saw ethnicity as a major stumbling block to the creation of a nation.

> To look from the tribe to a wider concept of human association is to be progressive. When this begins to happen, a Kenyan nation will be born. It will be an association, not of different tribal entities, but of individuals, free to journey to those heights of which they are capable. Nationalism, by breaking some tribal shells, will be a help. But nationalism should not in turn become another shackle. Nor should it be the end. The end should be man ultimately freed from fear, suspicion and parochial attitudes: free to develop and realise his full creative potential. (Ngugi 1972, p. 24)

Ngugi, then, like many others in the early 1960s, was grappling with the issues of ethnicity, individualism and nationalism, uneasy bedfellows at the best of times.

And yet, Ngugi's nationalist discourse is not entirely a European derivative, but the kind that gestures equally towards what the Indian scholar, Partha Chatterjee, calls 'a "modern" national culture that is nevertheless not Western' because it is located in a spiritual domain set outside colonial economy and statecraft (1993, p. 6). Chatterjee argues that Indian nationalism was janus-faced: looking both backward and forward at the same time. As a result it was neither willing to repudiate tradition nor to condemn those elements of colonialism from which it benefited. Ngugi's reconstruction of Agikuyu nationalism around the Agikuyu myth of creation, while at the same time embracing modernist notions of progress and development in his earlier texts, lends credence to Chatterjee's argument. These issues clearly form the foundation of Ngugi's earlier novels: *The River Between*, *Weep Not, Child* and *A Grain of Wheat*. To an extent, they continue to be of serious thematic concern in his subsequent novels in English and Gikuyu: *Petals of Blood*, *Devil on the Cross* and *Matigari*. Chatterjee, for example, concludes by making a distinction between elite nationalism as a gradualist attempt at change as opposed to the more radical 'war of movement', a distinction that Ngugi appears to be making in his latter novels. In the following chapters, I will explore Ngugi's earlier novels as texts written under the shadow of nationalism, whose creation involved a process of invention which was both contradictory and ambiguous. They were texts born in the throes of the problematic nationalist discourse of the early 1960s. The texts bear the scars of these contradictions and complex imaginings of nationalism.

The Postcolonial Phase

More recently, Ngugi wa Thiong'o has argued for a 'radical' reinterpretation of Kenya's history. The thrust of his argument is that Kenya's history has been distorted by the colonial writers and Kenya's professional or guild historians, trained and schooled in Western critical modes of thought.[5] At the heart of Ngugi's thesis is his contention that Kenya's working people, the workers and peasants, are marginalised, if not totally ignored, in the country's narrative history. Ngugi, therefore, seeks to intervene and to salvage the history of the subaltern[6] from the ruins of colonial plunder. Ngugi's intervention in this process of history-making, to use Cooper's words, strives to 'recover the lives of people who are forgotten in narratives of global exploitation and national mobilisation' (1994, p. 1516), all of which calls into question the very narratives themselves, indeed, the theoretical frameworks, and the subject positions of the colonialist and Kenyan historians implicated in the project. Ngugi's engagement with them is unequivocal, particularly in his novel, *Petals of Blood*:

> For there are many questions in our history which remain unanswered. Our present day historians, following on similar theories yarned out by defenders of imperialism, insist we only arrived here yesterday. Where went all the Kenyan people who used to trade with China, India, Arabia long long before Vasco da Gama came to the scene and on the strength of gunpowder ushered in an era of blood and terror and instability – an era that climaxed in the reign of imperialism over Kenya? But even then these adventures of Portuguese mercantilism were forced to build Fort Jesus,

showing that Kenyan people had always been ready to resist foreign control and exploitation. The story of this heroic resistance: who will sing it? Their struggles to defend their land, their wealth, their lives: who'll tell of it? What of their earlier achievements in production that had annually attracted visitors from China and India? (Ngugi 1977, p. 67)

Clearly, Ngugi rejects those historical archives akin to the West; he privileges resistance as the key plot element in African history; and he insists that the metanarrative of the nationalist victory has to be revised and reconstituted as the story of workers and peasants – history from below. Ngugi, to use Frederick Cooper's argument, takes the path many African scholars have taken by putting 'more emphasis on showing that Africans had history than on asking how Africans' history-making was implicated in establishing or contesting power' (Cooper 1994, p. 1528). For Ngugi, Kenyan history should be about the struggles of the subaltern, their resistance to colonial and neocolonial domination in the postcolonial state. This struggle crystallised itself in the Mau Mau anticolonial war, a struggle which should continue to inspire new resolves for freedom and dignity in Kenya's post-independence period. It is the narrative of the marginalised, Ngugi avers, which Kenya's pioneer historians like Ogot, Were, Muriuki and Ochien'g have suppressed.

And yet, can one safely argue that Ngugi has a monopoly over what constitutes Kenya's history simply because he privileges the history of the subaltern? Does not the privileging of one form of history also entail the suppression of another? To raise these questions is to ask questions of theoretical approaches to historical meaning: they are questions about the politics of historical interpretation. But they are also questions about the complexity of the theoretical perspective a writer adopts and how that choice enhances or limits his or her grasp of the subject under scrutiny.

The view taken in this book is that one can best understand history by exploring the politics of interpretation that inform a specific historical subject or phenomenon. Here I lean on

Hayden White's thesis that the significance of any historical narrative lies squarely in the politics that inform the interpretation of that subject and that 'interpretation presupposes politics as one of the conditions of its possibility as a social activity' (1987, p. 59). White's point is that historical apprehension is guided by specific interests that a given historical interpretation ultimately serves: 'Everyone recognizes that the way one makes sense of history is important in determining what politics one will credit as realistic, practicable, and socially responsible' (p. 73). In other words, there is no interpretation that is value free and, indeed, there can never be one interpretation of an historical subject. This does not mean, however, that every interpretation is adequate once the politics behind it have been established; one needs to explore the possibilities and the limits offered by a given interpretation or framework in exploring complex layers of knowledge.

Tracing Ngugi's Ideological Shift and Politics of Interpretation

What, then, is the possible nature of the politics behind Ngugi's interpretation of Kenyan history? How do we account for Ngugi's radical shift in his representation of Kenyan history in his postcolonial novels?[7] We can begin to account for Ngugi's ideological shift in terms of his biographical development. His exposure to the works of Marx and Fanon and the influence of a cohort group of African scholars while he was at Leeds University has been well documented.[8] Reading Fanon, in particular, must have transformed Ngugi's views on a number of issues, ranging from violence for liberation to the nature of neocolonialism. Fanon's criticism of the national bourgeoisie and his prediction of their neocolonial mentality find echoes in the postcolonial novels of Ngugi, as does Fanon's embracing of violence as a cardinal imperative in the decolonization process. Fanon's notion of the 'native poet' as the custodian of national culture and as educator is frequently echoed in Ngugi's essays (1972; 1981a).

But Ngugi was also influenced by the changes that were taking place in the Kenyan body politic following independence. The political scenario after independence was fraught with fears and frustrations, and disillusionment with Uhuru. As early as 1966, Ngugi's bitterness was beginning to show. In a note to *A Grain of Wheat* he observes: 'But the situation and the problems are real – sometimes too painfully real for peasants who fought the British yet who now see all that they fought for being put to one side.'

That Ngugi was increasingly frustrated by the new African government that could not deliver became abundantly clear (Ngugi 1981b). Like many of his contemporaries, Ngugi was beginning to suspect that for the national bourgeoisie (used loosely here to mean the African ruling class), independence did not entail fulfilling the fundamental promises the nationalist elite had made at the height of nationalism. As the historian Frederick Cooper observes,

> African novelists were the first intellectuals to bring before a wide public inside and outside the African continent profound questions about the corruption within postcolonial governments and the extent to which external domination persisted. Growing disillusionment made increasingly attractive the theories of 'underdevelopment', which located the poverty and weaknesses of 'peripheral' societies not in the colonial situation but in the more long-term process of domination within a capitalist world system. (1994, p. 1524)

Besides, the 1970s were marked by major debates on the nature of Kenya's political economy, and these were primarily within the related theoretical frameworks of dependency and underdevelopment. These debates sought to explain Kenya's political and economic predicament by linking colonial transformations and postcolonial development strategies.

Two major studies set the tone for the debate. E. A. Brett's *Colonialism and Underdevelopment in East Africa* (1973) and Colin Leys's *Underdevelopment in Kenya* (1974) spelt out the broad outlines of the underdevelopment and dependency perspectives, as well as their empirical manifestations in the context of Kenya's development processes. Focusing on the effects of colonial rule on economic change in Kenya, Brett

(1974, pp. 302–9) noted how colonialism catalysed Kenya's absorption into the world capitalist system while fostering economic measures that resulted in an imbalanced development.

Leys characterised Kenya's emergent economy as a neocolonial one with numerous structural constraints. He argued that Kenya's blend of neocolonialism was rooted in the transition from colonialism to independence, a transition which resulted in the transfer of political power to a regime based on the support of social classes closely linked to foreign capital. On the question of the evolution of an indigenous social class capable of spearheading national development, Leys noted that a middle class of educated Africans and new property owners became the core of the nationalist movement during the later phase of the colonial period. Yet this emerging class was unable to lead the socioeconomic transformation after independence because of its subordination to settler and international interests (Leys 1974).

The influence of Brett's and Leys's analyses of Kenya's political economy is evident in Ngugi's texts. For one, they reinforced Fanon's thesis on 'the pitfalls of national consciousness' whose reading, Ngugi argued, was central to the understanding of African literature (Ngugi 1986, p. 63). Meanwhile, on Ngugi's recommendation, Fanon's *The Wretched of the Earth*, Lenin's 'Imperialism, the Highest Stage of Capitalism' and Rodney's *How Europe Underdeveloped Africa* were compulsory reading in the literature department at Nairobi University.[9] All these books point to underdevelopment and dependency perspectives which Ngugi has passionately embraced since his days in Leeds. These perspectives continue to inform his texts, whether in Gikuyu or English.

Finally, I need to add that the continued existence of poverty and inequality in the postcolonial Kenyan society forced Ngugi to look back into history for a radical tradition, particularly after the banning of the Kenya People's Union (KPU), the only popular voice of the marginalised group in Kenya at the time (Furedi 1989, pp. 211–13). Fired by his admiration for Fanon's theory of 'revolutionary violence', Mau Mau was a sure source of instant inspiration for Ngugi;

it became the central link in the tradition of struggle among the subaltern and seems to be at the heart of Ngugi's sense of history in all his narratives.

The thrust of my argument in the chapters that follow is that, whereas in the earlier novels Ngugi captures the moral complexity of the historic war, in the later works the Mau Mau war is singularly seen as the ultimate expression of Kenya's anticolonial struggle – a class war against the colonising oppressor. It is the continuation of this war that Ngugi dramatises in his postcolonial novels. While in the earlier novels Ngugi expresses the possibilities of a syncretic culture, in the later novels he displays utter hostility towards anything deemed Western. In the postcolonial novels there is an increasing commitment to political, and more specifically Marxist ideals. The portrayal of heroes in Ngugi's postcolonial novels, for example, contrasts sharply with his portrayal of heroes in the first three novels. In the earlier novels Ngugi brings out the moral dilemma that confronts his heroes in their efforts to reconcile two antagonistic social groups in their society. If reconciliation, both to oneself and to community, is central to the structural organisation of the texts in the earlier novels, class conflict is central to the organisation of the later texts. If in the earlier novels character portrayal draws our attention to the complexity of issues raised in the narrative, in the later novels Ngugi tends towards a more mechanistic allegorising in which human and social issues are articulated through a linear representation of characters and history.

In the first chapter, I draw a sharper link and contrast between Ngugi's earlier works and the more contemporary works dealing directly with the independence period. I have used his response to the nationalist imaginings of the 1960s as a way of probing into the vexed historical representations in his works. I also locate his radical shift in the representation of Kenyan history in the 1970s and beyond in the sociohistorical debates of the period. Chapter 2 traces the changing nature of Ngugi's allegory and makes the point that there has been a major shift from the complex allegorising that we find in his earlier novels to the more traditionalist articulation of allegory as simple-minded in the postcolonial texts. The third chapter attempts to examine the narrative shifts from the more realistic modes of characterisation in the earlier novels to the overdetermined character types that we tend to associate with his more recent texts. The fourth chapter explores Ngugi's experimentation with popular forms as a major aspect of his new regime of 'decolonising' fiction. The focus is on the interface between orality and the written forms. The chapter attempts to show that although Ngugi's recourse to oral forms is more pronounced in his works, originally written in Gikuyu, his earlier novels have always been rooted in both popular mythology – the popular forms of the Agikuyu – and a fusion of modern Western conventions of writing. The fundamental difference between the two phases is that Ngugi anticipates differnt audiences at each phase. Chapter 5 traces Ngugi's treatment of gender relations in his texts and argues that romantic relationships act as major allegorical tropes in all his novels. The chapter explores how Ngugi relates these romantic relationships to the broader social concerns in his narrative. The radical shift in Ngugi's treatment of gender relations will be compared to his relatively more conservative readings of gender relations in the earlier novels. Finally, Chapter 6 focuses on Ngugi's portrayal of heroes, the marginalised groups and the community. I argue that Ngugi's portrayal of the community has tended to parallel his ideological convictions and shifts over the years. What is of interest here is how Ngugi negotiates the delicate balance between the individual and the community, the hero and the collective.

1

Ngugi's Concept of History

The Contradictions of Imagining the Nation in Earlier Works

In the early 1960s, when Ngugi was writing, the relationship between ethnicity and nationalism was clearly a vexed one. For one, the site for constituting the nation lay in reconstructing the past. But if one turned to history it had of necessity to be ethnic, an area of experience at which many writers tended to look with disdain. Alternatively, attempts to resolve this issue would seem to have involved the unwitting adoption of an anthropologically evolutionist position which posited ethnic polities as an earlier form of social organisation that would wither into the modern state.[1] Ngugi at this time clearly felt some irritation with the manifestations of ethnicity: 'To live on the level of race or tribe is to be less than whole. In order to live, a chick has to break out of the shell shutting it out from the light' (Ngugi 1972, p. 23). Ngugi's ideas on 'community' and African socialism did not make his case any better because these two became another terrain in which the 'tribe' and the nation could meld:

> The traditional concept of the African community should not be forgotten in our rush for western culture and political institutions which some regard as the ready-made solution to our problems. In the African way, the community serves the individual. And the individual finds the fullest development of his personality when he is working in and for the community as a whole. Land, food and wealth is for the community. In this community, culture belongs to all. For the rich and the poor, the foolish and the wise are all free to participate in the national life of the community in all its manifestations. Perhaps that is

15

what some have meant when they talk of African socialism. If so it is a worthy ideal. (Ngugi 1972, p. 25)

Ngugi's early novels, particularly *The River Between*, carry the ambiguities and contradictions that he is struggling to grapple with in the above passages. The construction of the Agikuyu community is, not surprisingly, complex and contradictory. On the most obvious level the community is meant to have an anthropological feel to it. Words like 'custom', 'ancient', 'traditions', 'tribe' and 'ritual' abound and immediately create some anthropological texture. The precolonial history of the polity is constituted almost exclusively through a religious myth of origin and the whole issue of 'tribal tradition' is collapsed into one single institution – circumcision, which is seen as a fulcrum of the community. The influence of Kenyatta's *Facing Mount Kenya*, which Ngugi has described as 'a living example of ... integrative culture' (Ngugi 1972, p. 7), is most evident here. Kenyatta makes a meal out of Agikuyu female circumcision and it is significant that the plot of *The River Between*, which centres around the Agikuyu history of the 1920s and 1930s, crystallises around the Protestant mission's opposition to female circumcision.

Another meaning of ethnicity in the text emerges from Ngugi's attempt to portray the community as an anachronistic, ossified force. In the opening chapter of the novel, the two communities in the novel are heavily associated with geography in a way that is almost geological: the two ridges on which the communities live are like 'sleeping lions which never woke. They just slept, the big deep sleep of their Creator' (Ngugi 1972, p. 1). Related to this strand is the constant emphasis on the secretiveness of 'the tribe' which is constituted by a 'secret language of the hills', by unspecified 'tribal secrets' and 'hidden things'. This mysteriousness is transposed onto the shadowy Kiama and its penultimate showdown with Waiyaki (Chapter 23); the constant emphasis on murkiness is transposed onto the organisation and the 'tribalism' that it represents. On one level, then, ethnicity signifies anthropological curiosity and obsolescence, a strand of meaning which incorporates Kabonyi and Kiama who refuse to heed the calls of the 'modernisers', act with impure motive and favour a type of 'backward-looking primary resistance' in an age of 'modernisation'. This model of inward-looking nationalism arguably owes something to a brand of early 1960s African historiography associated with people like Robinson and Gallagher (see Ranger 1968, pp. 437–8).

And yet, the tensions associated with ethnicity and its meaning are numerous. Ethnicity must bear the weight of being ossified and backward-looking; it must also refract a sentimentalised construction of precolonial society as an organic whole. And finally, ethnicity in certain parts must stand for itself and the nation simultaneously. This strand of investing the 'tribe' with the meaning of the nation is perhaps not pronounced but is mediated obliquely.

In addition, an implied familiarity with the landscape ('The two ridges' rather than 'two ridges') and certain specified geographical markers can be read to signify 'nationness'. However, this is not without its contradictions and the narrator, for example, vacillates between an implied familiarity with the landscape and acting as a guide to a foreign reader: 'Unless you are careful, you could easily lose your way in the hills' (Ngugi 1965, p. 8). This narrative duality can, I think, be related back to the contradiction of ethnicity as anthropological curiosity and the ethnic polity as partial metaphor for the nation. However, this myth of origin, as we shall see in Ngugi's later texts, is replaced by the imagery of dispossession, of loss, of landlessness, of longing for the 'lost lands' to be restored. In later texts Mau Mau becomes a major symbol around which the various aspects of Kenyan history cohere.

With regard to nationalism, the depiction is more complex than that of ethnicity. In the opening chapter of the novel, alongside portrayals of the ossified ethnic polity, we are presented with glimpses of the 'proto-nationalists', those who seek to shake off the claustrophobic secrecy of the 'tribe' in favour of some wider social aggregate. In a brief historical pageant, we are presented with Mugo wa Kibiro, a 'great Agikuyu seer of old', Kamiri, the sorcerer and Wachiori, 'a great warrior' (Ngugi 1965, p. 2). These belong to the select band of people who 'went out. Those who had the courage to look beyond their present content to a life and land beyond, were the select few sent by Murungu to save a people in their hour of need' (p. 3). But it is also made clear that these messiahs will not be hailed in their own time and will instead be given short shrift by the people of the 'ancient', 'isolated', 'sleeping' ridges. This line of proto-nationalists includes Chege, Waiyaki's father, and his prophecies about the corrosive effects of colonialism will also be ignored. This lineage of outward-looking men gets its fullest realisation in Waiyaki, the fully-fledged, youthful, nationalist protagonist. His credentials as a nation-builder lie in the language that he speaks which is that of the 1960s 'moderniser': education, unity, advancement, growth, development, patriotism, high ideals, reconciliation, tolerance, enlightenment, mission and vision are the words that form the backbone of his lexicon. The bright boy of Siriana, meeting people from other parts of Kenya, he is the ideal embodiment of the nation. And yet Waiyaki has of necessity to be constituted through a series of ambiguities and ambivalences. On the one hand, he embodies a type of pure nationalism: 'Kinuthia [his friend] was convinced that Waiyaki was the best man to lead people, not only to a new light through education, but also to new opportunities and areas of self-expression through political independence' (p. 118). Part of this project involves an attempt to escape or free himself from the 'ritual demand of the tribe' (p. 121), while another part entails an endeavour to try and modernise the 'tribe' through education. On the other hand, Waiyaki has to try and inscribe his nationalism with some vestige of ethnicity and his attempts to do so are couched in the following terms: 'A people's traditions could not be swept away overnight. That way lay disintegration. Such a tribe would have no roots, for a people's roots were in their traditions going back to the past, the very beginning, Gikuyu and Mumbi' (p. 141). Waiyaki, in attempting to articulate the essence of the ethnic 'tribe', can only do so in nationalist terms of a myth of origin.

Evidently, Ngugi's maiden text, *The River Between*, was written under the shadow of nationalism whose creation involved a process of invention which was both contradictory and ambiguous. It was a text born in the throes of the problematic nationalist discourse of the early 1960s. The text bears the scars of these contradictions. For example, there are two compelling historical omissions which relate directly to the writer's attempts to give a picture of an organic and united ethnic community, threatened by a foreign force. The first omission relates to the independent school movement which fell under two broad organisational umbrellas: Kikuyu Independent Schools Association and the Kikuyu Karing'a (Pure) Educational Association. The movement began in the early 1920s and formed part of a more general response to a variety of pressures that were making themselves felt in Agikuyu societies. On the one hand, colonial tax and labour demands sharpened drastically as the colonial state intervened to reconstruct settler agriculture which up until the end of the First World War had been a rather ramshackle affair. On the other hand, many ordinary Agikuyu faced growing landlessness as the chiefly class of Agikuyu notables consolidated their land holdings, often at the direct expense of their tenants. Various political organisations capitalised on this discontent and these movements had links with the independent school associations. These associations directed their attention specifically to mission education and by their separatist strategies attempted to focus on and remedy the quantitative and qualitative shortcomings of church schooling (see Anderson 1970, Chapter 8; Ranger 1965, pp. 55–85).

But exactly what is the substance of Ngugi's historical deviation? His deviation lies in the fact that the novel contains not a single reference to an independent church movement. And yet any account of the period will tell you that independent school movements invariably went hand in hand with an independent church grouping. The relationship between the two was always complex but seemed to hinge around a symbiosis: a church could attract schoolgoers and a school, church members. In addition, the independent churches could provide an avenue for advancement which white-dominated mission institutions blocked. The independent churches attracted a large-scale popular following and have remained an important feature of Kenya's socioreligious landscape (Gertzel *et al.* 1969).

The second omission in the text concerns the depiction of Agikuyu society, which is highly artificial. Throughout the novel it is their isolation that is stressed and one of the Kiama's aims is to protect this insularity. In addition, the populace of the novel constitutes a subsistence society that does not seem to trade and there is only one brief mention of Indian traders. This isolation does bear some resemblance to Kenyan history and, through its broad outline, Ngugi was probably attempting to capture the relative lateness and suddenness of British colonisation since the Agikuyu, unlike societies further south, did not experience centuries of European contact through slave and ivory trades. All this notwithstanding, to posit an isolated community in the Central Highlands of the 1920s is noteworthy, particularly when one bears in mind that up until 1918, 75 per cent of export commodities and produce was produced by peasants (Brett 1973, p. 176). The second reinterpretation involves the *sociological* texture of the community which in the text appears to be entirely homogenous. As pointed out above, the Agikuyu community by the 1920s was becoming increasingly stratified as intruding settler agriculture and colonial administration exacerbated precolonial patterns of landholders and tenants.

It is in his next two novels, *Weep Not, Child* and *A Grain of Wheat*, that Ngugi manages to resolve some of the nationalist contradictions that are most manifest in *The River Between*. Although Ngugi's abhorrence of ethnicity remains a major subtext in the two novels, the nature of his historical invention is more nuanced than it is in *The River Between*. In both texts Ngugi is at pains to foreground the necessity for struggling towards a Kenyan nation without either falling back on some organic ethnic community or deleting histories of conflict and difference among the Agikuyu community. For texts that revolve around land alienation and the Mau Mau war, it is significant that Ngugi uses ethnicity more as a template for his nationalist imaginings rather than as a negative force that must be obliterated.

The texts still revolve around the Agikuyu myth of origin as founder of the Agikuyu nation. Land, which is at the heart of the struggle in the two texts, was designated by God, Murungu, to the Agikuyu founders: Gikuyu and Mumbi. If political freedom in Kenya became synonymous with repossession of the land, the spiritual and moral justification for this quest for freedom lies in the fact that this land is linked to the spiritual right of the people, the Agikuyu. The land was God-given; it was entrusted to them by their legendary ancestors as a form of covenant between God and his people. If the Agikuyu from time immemorial have used land as a rallying symbol and a metaphor for cohesion between the living and the dead, now Ngugi posits land as a metaphor for change and conflict. With the advent of colonialism, land which hitherto united the Agikuyu now divides them. Although they are convinced that the land has to be recovered, they are divided by the means of recovery. The fundamental question confronting a nationalist writer like Ngugi is how one invents a nationalist history in the face of divisions engendered by colonialism? How does one begin to imagine the nation if the very vehicle for its foundational unity, land, now divides the nation? In fact, how does one articulate the ambivalent relationship between land, ethnicity, individualism and nationalism?

To begin with, the strand of inward-looking ethnicity that we find in *The River Between*, chiefly represented in the Kiama, is almost deleted in *Weep Not, Child*. Instead we are presented with the Agikuyu community in the throes of change; it is a society in turmoil and conflict. Divided, as it were, between the settler colonialists and the natives, the homeguards and the *ahoi* (squatters), Ngugi's basic dilemma is how to constitute a purely nationalist discourse in the face of these divisions. Of course the easy way out is to repress the divisions and to gesture towards a unitary Kenyan nation in keeping with the nationalist discourses of the 1960s. This option is so real and tempting that once again Ngugi resorts to the image of the 'modern' nationalist builder and its lexicon – a portrait almost reminiscent of Waiyaki. Just as in *The River Between*, the school in *Weep Not, Child* continues to provide the neutral space for imagining the nation and the young Njoroge and

Mwihaki are its most striking icons. Both in their language and vision they gesture towards a future Kenyan nation free of strife, ethnic divisions and even racial hatred. The school for Ngugi is a microcosm of diversity, peace and the ideal nation: 'Njoroge at times wished the whole school was like this. This seemed a little paradise, a paradise where children from all walks of life and of different religious faiths could work together without any consciousness. Many people believed the harmony in the school came because the headmaster was a strange man who was severe with everyone, black and white' (Ngugi 1964, p. 115).

The significance of the school for Njoroge lies in the fact that it can bring together people of diverse backgrounds and cultures: the *ahoi* and the homeguards; the settler and the native. For Ngugi the school, a colonialist institution in the form of education, could be appropriated in the service of black freedom. In a significant way, Njoroge continues the modernist lexicon of Waiyaki – education for liberation – and like Waiyaki, he ends up dejected and disillusioned because of the complexity of the moment which cannot be understood purely in such simplistic terms like unity, sacrifice, education and progress.

It is in *A Grain of Wheat*, generally regarded as Ngugi's most accomplished novel, that he gives his most complex picture of the nationalist politics of liberation. Written less than four years after Kenya's independence, it is both a novel of anticipation in its historical setting and a novel that draws attention to the present by interrogating the nationalist meta-narratives of the triumphal takeover of the nation-state, while at the same time gesturing towards the future. As Caminero-Santangelo writes, the text 'represents the possibility of betrayal of the ideals and goals of the national liberation movement by those who have gained power in the newly independent Kenya, precisely because they are still controlled by self-interest and by conceptions of social-political relations' (Caminero-Santangelo 1998, p. 142). Unlike Ngugi's first two novels, it deviates from the modernist project embraced by both Waiyaki and Njoroge. Where education provided the space for imagining a new Kenyan nation in *The River Between* and *Weep Not, Child*, in *A Grain of Wheat* the Mau Mau war becomes the major icon around which national identity has to be built. In this sense it provides a major link to Ngugi's later novels.

The Mau Mau war, the anticolonial struggle, provides Ngugi with the space to imagine the birth of a new Kenya. Here, Ngugi also resorts to oral mythology to naturalise the process. Colonial invasion of Kenya had been prophesied by the Agikuyu seer of old, Mugo wa Kibiro. The seeds of nationalist war of liberation also go back into the people's history. Warriors led by Waiyaki took up arms during the primary resistance to colonial penetration, thereby planting seeds of sacrifice and resistance that would later find their ultimate expression in the Mau Mau war. Waiyaki is followed by Harry Thuku who founds the Young Kikuyu Association which by 1923 had provided the base for broadening the party into a nationalist movement. By the time Kenyatta emerges on the scene, the party's base had broadened and we are told that the party's 'influence stretched from one horizon touching the sea to the other resting on the great Lake' (Ngugi 1967, p. 11). In the meeting that Kenyatta was to address, the writer is at pains to stress that among the speakers, 'there was also a Luo speaker from Nyanza showing that the Party had broken barriers between tribes' (p. 14). In the same meeting Kihika talks of 'the call of a nation in turmoil' even if it means going against a brother (p. 15).

In a typical nationalist idiom, Ngugi underscores the centrality of unity and necessity of sacrifice for a better Kenya. The notion of sacrifice is embodied in Kihika and, more importantly, in Ngugi's endorsement of the Mau Mau violence – a major shift from the first two texts in which education provided the neutral space between the forest fighters on the one hand and the homeguards and the colonial settlers on the other. The nationalist perspective of the text hinges on sacrifice, sowing of seeds which would die in order to bear grain. Indeed, the first two chapters dramatise this sacrifice, with the ultimate price paid by Kihika: 'although killed, the party, however, remained alive and grew, as people put it, on the wounds of those Kihika left behind' (Ngugi 1967, pp. 18–19). And although Ngugi's *A Grain of Wheat* and to an extent *Weep Not, Child* draw attention to the grand themes of a nationalist text *par excellence*, unity and sacrifice to freedom, they nevertheless deviate from the orthodox portrayal in a very fundamental way.

Deviation from the Standard Nationalist Portrayal of Guerrilla War

While both *Weep Not, Child* and *A Grain of Wheat* acknowledge the sacrifice of many Kenyan heroes and indeed celebrate it, and while they both gesture towards similar nationalist projects that *The River Between* anticipates, they nevertheless make a radical shift away from the standard orthodox portrayal of a liberation war. They do this in several ways. By examining the moral choices that a war of liberation imposes on people, they are able to show that both sides – the nationalist fighters and collaborators, blacks and settlers – confronted difficult moral choices and dilemmas. In terms of their social ideology the texts do not privilege collective experience over individual subjectivity, but draw our attention to how lives of individual characters and groups were affected by the war of liberation.

In *Weep Not, Child*, for example, Ngugi is keen to draw attention to the disruptive nature of a liberation war. The emergency period is presented as disruptive, not just of the social structure of the Agikuyu society, but also of the lives of the colonial settlers, chiefly represented in Howlands. The war not only affects the ideal African family of Ngotho that is torn apart, but it also affects the lives of collaborators like Jacobo. Above all, it is most disruptive of the lives of innocent children, Njoroge and Mwihaki. And far from being a unifying phenomenon, the liberation war unleashes new forces of change. It leads to a realignment of power relations and shifts in traditional roles and authority. The inaction of the elders leads to a crisis of authority in Ngotho's household. Boro, Ngotho's son, having lost respect for him, now wants to administer oath. Ngotho's intervention and interest in the Mau Mau war is not entirely motivated by land alienation. He is primarily motivated by a basic loss of authority brought by the youthful Mau Mau fighters. He cannot accept oath administered by his son, Boro. The war thus engenders generational conflict, thereby shifting the traditional power base away from the elders to the youth. Ngotho is interested in the war, only to the extent that it will restore his authority. He is faced with a moral dilemma: whether to defend his power base or to follow the younger generation; to capitulate to their recently acquired authority or to resist. Ironically, even for Boro, the struggle has been so ugly that he has lost interest in its recovery. The struggle for land has been so violently bloody that he has 'lost too many of those whom [he] loved for the land to mean much to [him]' (Ngugi 1964, p. 102). The violent aspect of the struggle has only served to alienate Boro further and further away from his family and from its ultimate goal – land restoration.

In *A Grain of Wheat*, Ngugi points to the difficulty that one is likely to encounter in trying to give an historic account of a liberation war and its effects on ordinary individuals. Here, again, Ngugi is at his most poignant in drawing attention to the disruptive nature of war and the moral choices it imposes on people. In a definite departure from orthodox nationalist narrative, Ngugi is reluctant to valorise sacrifice and hints at the fact that the nationalist triumph is in fact a historical farce. The difficulty of identifying the hero of the novel that many critics have alluded to points to his reluctance to celebrate war heroes. Instead he subverts the standard nationalist ideology of hero worship by giving voice to all those who are implicated in the struggle, directly or indirectly. He privileges the voice of the peasants, often deleted in grand nationalist narratives in favour of the 'elite'. Isolated and away from the political rhetoric in Nairobi, the Mau Mau war becomes for the rural peasants distasteful because it has failed to deliver. The Uhuru celebrations are met with apprehension by the peasants of Thabai. Significantly, the outcome of the Mau Mau war does not coincide with the expectations of the peasants. Instead, the narrative hints directly at the incessant betrayal, almost embedded in the practice and process of war from its inception. The individual themes of betrayal translate into political themes of betrayal. If in the later texts Ngugi seems to isolate patriots from traitors, in *A Grain of Wheat* the line between the two is blurred and the narrative calls for political scepticism and cynicism towards heroism and hero worship. Retrospection and introspection, as opposed to uncritical celebration of triumphant ideologies that marked the history of resistance in the 1960s, are called for if the dream of a new Kenyan nation has to be realised. It is for this reason that all characters, ranging from Gikonyo to Mumbi, Mugo to General R, come to the realisation that the calamity of the war is real and has left an indelible mark in their psyche and consequently everything else is seen through a filter of a disturbed mind – the very evidence of the ravages of war. Not even the guerrillas are spared in this retrospection and introspection, because their atrocities are not disguised. This is the ultimate historical truth that confronts the young Njoroge in *Weep Not, Child* when he remarks: '"I thought the Mau Mau was on the side of the black people" ' (Ngugi 1964, p. 83).

In *A Grain of Wheat* Ngugi also deconstructs the primordial national essence or character which he left unresolved in *The River Between*. In the new 'postcolonial' Kenyan nation, the belief that the age of colonialism is over because the British have left is likely to undermine the interests of a majority of Kenyans since it will mask the need for resistance against neo-colonialism. While *A Grain of Wheat* is certainly concerned with the effects of underdevelopment under colonialism, the danger at the moment of decolonisation is that despite the departure of the British, colonial and capitalist structures and ideology will continue to shape Kenyans' perceptions. Colonialism continues under black colonial masters working with white settlers and European powers. Kenyans are, therefore, likely to embrace the colonial structures which will continue to underdevelop their society. It is this theme of underdevelopment and dependency syndrome that dominates Ngugi's later novels dealing squarely with the post-colonial state.

The Later Novels

The thrust of Ngugi's narrative concerns over the last two decades has been the struggle for *Matunda ya Uhuru* – the Fruits of Freedom. It has been a project directed at decolonisation, embodying the varied processes of political independence, national liberation and people's revolution. It has been a project focused on the making of democracy – the struggle for social change in the postcolonial state – and therefore a useful intervention in the postcolonial discourses in Kenya.

This section is both a critique and a demonstration of Ngugi's sense of history as a major voice in the struggle for sociopolitical change in the postcolonial state in Kenya. I seek to demonstrate here that Ngugi's sense of history is closely linked to his politics of interpretation – to his political project *vis-à-vis* the postcolonial body politic in Kenya – and that his texts depicting postcolonial Kenya are best understood if placed against the contradictory flux of postcolonial discourses in Kenya that I have discussed in the introductory chapter. It seeks to demonstrate that although Ngugi's novels have been perceived largely as discourses on cultural decolonisation, they involve the quest for a new sociopolitical order. In this quest, Ngugi foregrounds land as a recurring economic and political metaphor in the decolonisation process in Kenya; he critiques the African elite that captured state power at independence as mere watchdogs of Western capitalism; and, of course, he raises his pet theme of cultural imperialism and strategies for the African revolution. A dialogical reading of Ngugi's texts, as I will argue with regard to his later novels, links his concept of history to dependency theory discourses in Kenya and Fanon's conceptualisation of the postcolonial revolution in Africa (Brett 1973; Fanon 1967; Kitching 1977 and 1980; Langdon 1977 and 1981; Leys 1974). The silences – the suppressed histories in Ngugi's texts – are invariably linked to the tendency within a dependency framework to suppress local and the more specific social conflicts in society.

According to Ngugi, the single most important virtue in traditional African society was common ownership of land which was worked by all for the common good. When the white colonialists appropriated the land, conflict and general suffering ensued. Ngugi's treatment of these issues suggests that Kenya's precolonial history was devoid of any turmoil and conflict until the advent of colonialism. Thus, one might deduce that, for Ngugi, the history of conflict in Africa is the history of colonialism and how it affected the African populace. Ngugi is therefore at pains to document colonial injustices in most of his works. In works that deal with the postcolonial experience, the colonial context always serves as a major backdrop against which the postcolonial experiences (read neocolonial) are examined.

The colonial state for Ngugi is always allegorical of the postcolonial state. The most outstanding image in his recreation of the colonial and postcolonial experience is land. Land, for Ngugi, remains an important metaphor for explicating Kenya's past and present history in his later novels. Land is depicted as a metaphor for life; it is a source of livelihood. Land is both a metaphor for struggle and the physical space for political contest in virtually all the writer's works. A metaphor for flux, land is the agent for social change and economic mobility: the agent for social transformation within society. Indeed, the theme of resistance to and collaboration with the colonial institutions is linked to this metaphor. Thus the nature of the colonial and neocolonial experience in Kenya can be understood only through the contradictory and multiple functions and conflicts that land generates for Ngugi. The solution to social conflict is, by implication, only possible when land is shared and worked by all.

Ngugi's interest in the plight of the peasantry as a dispossessed group seems to echo Fanon's understanding of the peasantry both as the most exploited group and as having the potential to provide revolutionary change in the postcolonial state (Fanon 1967, pp. 85–118). It is significant that Ilmorog, which is both a symbol of land in its most ideal state – land as communal property and a home of the peasantry – is one of the major settings of the two novels, *Petals of Blood* and *Devil on the Cross*. And with the advent of colonialism and capital investment in Ilmorog, we witness economic deprivation of peasants and workers. They are forced to live off the slave wages of African landowners and African businessmen in partnership with multinational companies that have recently taken over Ilmorog. The deprivation of the peasants of Ilmorog contrasts sharply with the wealth of colonial settlers and African farmers. Independence does not usher in any comfort or economic gains for peasants and workers; it is the same group of loyalists, otherwise called 'homeguards' by Ngugi, that emerges as the beneficiaries of Uhuru. Ilmorog is, therefore, a physical manifestation of the contradictory presence of poverty and capital in Kenya. Thus the ills of the colonial state are simply reproduced in the post-colonial state. For example, Kimeria, who betrayed Abdulla and Ndinguri during the Mau Mau war, is the new hero of political independence. Through Waweru – the landowner – and his father Brother Ezekiel, Ngugi demonstrates that the exploitation of deprived peasants and workers becomes a family business.

The 'mutilation' of land by both colonial and postcolonial oppressor is done through the aid of religious, cultural and educational institutions which instil and perpetuate mental slavery of the oppressed and buttress the interests of the oppressor (Ngugi 1972, p. 31). Christian religion is used to inflict what Ngugi calls a 'psychological wound ... on the whole generation' (Ngugi 1973, p. xii). Ngugi's position is that religion is a tool for oppressing workers. In *Petals of Blood*, Waweru is portrayed as a man who propagates Christianity because it is rewarding to him and his family. Reverend Waweru is said to have taken refuge in religion at the time of Kenya's struggle for independence, denouncing all anticolo-nial activities such as Mau Mau oathing rituals as the devil's work. In addition, cultural and educational institutions are seen too by Ngugi as tools for mental slavery; they are used to perpetuate mental captivity in the postcolonial state. Criticism of naked imitation of Western values is chiefly represented by the native bourgeoisie in *Devil on the Cross*. Here, Kihaahu is a typical example of the alienated black who aspires to be white in all respects – he changes his name to a white one. Indeed, Ngugi's satire on Kenyan bourgeois attitudes is best expressed by Kihaahu's nursery school scheme whose success is associated with everything white (Ngugi 1982, p. 113).

The love for Western goods reaches a level of absurdity when Gitutu suggests that they should import air (Ngugi 1982, p. 107). Thus, for the African elite, goods acquire their true value only if and when they are imported. In this way, the writer is providing a salient critique of the postcolonial economy in which the raw materials are exported from the colonies, manufactured in the West and brought back as finished products. From Ngugi's point of view, the national bourgeoisie is much worse than Fanon's assessment of them as entrepreneurial because they are mere consumers helping to entrench trade imbalances between the poor and the rich Western countries, while perpetuating the poverty of their own people. In *Petals of Blood*, Ngugi depicts the displacement of Abdulla and Wanja of Theng'eta Breweries as a conspiracy between rich African financiers and their foreign allies. Ngugi seems to point to a conspiracy between the African leadership in the postcolonial state and international capital as the major cause of this cultural and economic impoverishment. They are a decadent class that perpetuates contempt for African values.

To recapitulate, Ngugi seems to be suggesting that the churches, the African leadership, the local and foreign capital are in an undeclared pact to exploit Kenya's resources to the detriment of the poor masses. Ngugi seems to be echoing Fanon's critique of the national bourgeoisie as a shallow and uncreative lot, a class which works at naked imitation of its European counterpart without helping the lot of the African masses because it simply cannot sever its links with the Western bourgeoisie, which it serves. In *Devil on the Cross*, Ngugi is apparently dramatising the fate of this class through the use of the fantastic and the unbelievable by putting on show characters who boast about their cleverness and their cunning in the ways in which they steal from the people and they serve their foreign masters.

But as a response to this deplorable state of affairs in the postcolonial state in Kenya, Ngugi suggests that workers do resist the postcolonial leadership's naked robbery. He does not just create the possibility of revolt and a revolution, but demonstrates that Kenya's history has never been a one-sided story of the victorious oppressor, but that it has been characterised by heroic resistance of ordinary people. As Karega, the main protagonist in *Petals of Blood*, says:

The true lesson of history was this: that the so-called victims, the poor, the downtrodden, the masses, had always struggled with their spears and arrows, with their hands and songs of courage and hope, to end their oppression and exploitation. (Ngugi 1977, p. 303)

Ngugi reinforces the possibilities of revolt in his creation of characters who are positively disposed to revolutionary transformation within the society.

But Ngugi's position in relation to the revolutionary force in Kenya remains blurred. It is not consistent, as he seems to shift his opinion in all three novels from the peasants' political consciousness to the proletariat as the custodians of the political future. At times, Ngugi seems to be espousing Fanon's theory on the role of the peasants as a decisive force in Ilmorog, exemplified by the march of the Ilmorog peasants to the city in *Petals of Blood*.[2] And yet he shifts to the alternative of the trade union as a vehicle for change. Karega the brewery worker and trade union leader embodies Ngugi's shift. After organising with the peasants the march to Nairobi, he moves on to build a union and organise strikes in the industrial world, for better wages and better working conditions.

Ngugi seems to anticipate a socialist revolution through organised labour. The description of the desperate conditions of the workers shows that Ngugi moves away from Fanon's theory on the urban proletariat as a pampered lot (Fanon 1967, p. 86). He does not, however, create a distinction between the urban working class and the poorer peasantry. In *Petals of Blood*, neither the poor peasantry nor the factory workers own the means of production, and those who own some form of business like Wanja and Abdulla are displaced by big capital.

Ngugi's message would seem to suggest the formation of a revolutionary movement consisting of committed intellectuals such as Karega and the people, whether they are peasants or workers in factories. It is this same vision that we find in *Devil on the Cross* where Muturi rallies the Ilmorog workers to invade the Devil's feast. Muturi also tries to create political awareness among the workers by organising them to demand higher pay in Boss Kihara's company. Apparently, the role of trade unionism as a tool to build a socialist state appeals to Ngugi. This would seem to be Ngugi's primary discourse on resistance in *Petals of Blood* and *Devil on the Cross* as reflected in his portrayal of Karega and Muturi.

In these two novels, the possibility of violent resistance is an undeveloped sub-text. We have the constant reference to Mau Mau as the ultimate symbol of national liberation in Kenya.[3] Resistance through armed struggle is pushed further through a symbolic gesture in the action of Wariinga in killing Gitahi 'to save many other people, whose lives will not be ruined by words of honey and perfume' (Ngugi 1982, p. 253). But the theme of violence in Kenya's history is best dramatised in *Matigari*. According to the hero, Matigari, the oppressor cannot be rooted out without violence (Ngugi 1987, p. 131). Indeed, Ngugi seems to be suggesting that armed struggle should supplement trade union resistance. What Ngaruro wa Kiriro, the worker leader in *Matigari*, is doing in organising workers only finds its concrete expression in the violent attempt by Matigari to win back his house and land, first taken by Settler Williams and later passed on to John Boy and family.

Ngugi seems to be saying that the history of the postcolonial state in Kenya is one in which peasants and workers grow poorer, where women are exploited, where the national cultures of the people are trampled upon by a powerless bourgeoisie – alienated to the extent of thinking in terms of and blindly serving European values. The answer to all these problems is the concerted struggle of peasant workers through mass mobilisation, trade union movements and violent resistance aimed at defeating, as Ngugi himself puts it, 'imperialism and creat[ing] a higher system of democracy and socialism in alliance with all the other peoples of the world' (1986, pp. 29–30).

Suppression and Silences

Ngugi's understanding of the historical processes in Kenya is too deeply embedded in dependency theory to allow for a nuanced understanding of the complex colonial and postcolonial experience in Kenya. Ngugi's articulation of Kenyan history from a dependency theory perspective cannot allow him to deal with specific contradictions and local divisions within Kenya, and Ngugi is therefore forced to suppress certain histories.

What then are these ellipses in Ngugi's narrative? One of the major gaps concerns Ngugi's linear representation of the Mau Mau as a monolithic nationalist movement devoid of any contradictions. If the colonialists gave an extremely one-sided and perhaps an entirely biased historical version of the Mau Mau war, it would seem to me that Ngugi, in his anxiety to counter this, has tended to give a wholly romantic picture of the Mau Mau war. In Ngugi's postcolonial novels, Mau Mau is appropriated to legitimise the anti-imperialist struggle in the postcolonial Kenyan political economy. In the process, Ngugi gives Mau Mau 'new' ideological attributes: it was class-based in both its aims of eradicating capitalism and establishing a socialist Kenya; it united all Kenyan peasants and workers; it was not just a regional revolt, but a nationalist revolution with a clear vision for the postcolonial state.

In his invention of the Mau Mau, Ngugi presupposes the existence of a collective consciousness among the peasantry and the working class in Kenya, the kind of consciousness that engendered their struggle against colonialism (Ngugi and Mugo 1976, Preface). Thus, for Ngugi, all Kenyan peasants and workers had the same nationalist goals in their resistance to colonial rule, and the same interests continue to inspire their resistance in the postcolonial state. What we have is a situation in which the intellectual writer subsumes what may be local or regional interests of the peasants into national or class issues.[4]

For Ngugi, the Mau Mau war was not just a localised anti-colonial resistance waged by a section of the Agikuyu, but a national phenomenon and a point at which the schismatic segments of Kenyan history are summoned and ordered into a coherent centre. Thus, the ethnic interests and dimensions are suppressed, and the Mau Mau fighters are given a class vision. Ngugi is therefore silent on the diverse and often conflicting layers of consciousness that might have informed the historic Mau Mau. For example, the Mau Mau songs testify to their simultaneous commitment to the house of Mumbi, to the Gods of mount Kerenyaga, to liberating the land, and also to a future Kenya ruled by Kenyatta (Kinyatti 1980; Kabira and Mutahi 1988). The songs point to layers of consciousness and complex layers of knowledge about the Mau Mau that cannot be conflated into a monolithic narrative of the Mau Mau as Ngugi attempts to do in most of his works.

The view here is that the production of Mau Mau history has always fallen within the terrain of power contest (Odhiambo 1991, pp. 300–7; Cohen 1986, p. 48), and as long as the contestants continue to appropriate Mau Mau either to subvert or to legitimise the politics of the day, the image of Mau Mau can never be as absolute as Ngugi attempts to present in his narrative. Over the years, the Mau Mau war has survived as an ambivalent phenomenon in colonial and postcolonial Kenyan politics. It is a symbol to be appropriated, and at times negated, for political gains.

In this game of political manipulation, the Mau Mau war veterans have tended to serve sectarian, conservative and ethnic interests. Kenyatta suppressed the role played by the Mau Mau fighters on the eve of independence and declared that all Kenyans fought for Uhuru. In 1966, when Oginga Odinga broke ranks with Kenyatta and formed an opposition party, Kenyatta deemed it fit to rally Mau Mau veterans, as the custodians of the Agikuyu interest, against the perceived threat from Odinga's Luo-dominated Kenya Peoples Union (Furedi 1989, p. 208). When Bildad Kaggia, a former Mau Mau detainee, joined KPU to help Odinga to articulate the interests of the Mau Mau guerrillas, especially on the question of land, he received no support from former guerrillas. Ethnic interest took precedence (Maloba 1993, p. 175). As recently as 1992, the current president of Kenya, Daniel Arap Moi, rallied an estimated 3,000 former Mau Mau fighters against the main opposition parties fighting for the restoration of democracy. Ironically, in this shrewd political ploy, Moi, who was perceived by many as the lackey of the colonial regime, reaped the spoils of Mau Mau heroism in order to subvert democracy. In the typical language of Ngugi and wa Kinyatti, the former guerrillas dismissed certain members of the opposition as 'collaborators' and 'sons of homeguards' (*The Weekly Review*, 24 July 1992, p. 18).

Another major gap in Ngugi's narrative is his attempt to link the conditions of the colonial state with those of the postcolonial state. Ngugi assumes a linear tradition and continuity in the anti-imperialist struggle. He contends that the fight against colonialism and capitalism in post-independent Kenya is a continuation of the Kenyan people's struggle which stretches back to the primary resistance against colonialism. We are given a glorified picture of the heroic resistance, by Kenyan peasants, to foreign invasion. Indeed, this linear approach to historical interpretation also overlooks the possibility that there may be no link between the militant nationalist struggles of the 1950s and the anti-imperialist forces in the post-independence Kenya. And yet, Ngugi seems to suggest that the same continuity persists in the camp of the collaborators who seem to reproduce themselves in a geometric manner right from the colonial period into post-colonial Kenya.

It seems to me that Ngugi does not succeed in capturing the ambivalent relationship between the colonial state and the loyalists. In Ngugi's texts, there seems to be no tension between the loyalists, on the one hand, and the colonial state, on the other. He depicts the relationship as one of mutual trust and dependence. A good example of this relationship is Ngugi's portrayal of Waweru and Ndikita in *Petals of Blood* and his treatment of John Boy in *Matigari*. All the characters seem to have a linear and unproblematic relationship with the colonial regime, with their loyalty to the colonial state being absolute. This relationship of absolute dependence is best dramatised in Wariinga's nightmare in which the colonising devil is crucified upon the cross, and he ends up being rescued by the local comprador – symbolically signalling the emergence of neocolonialism (Ngugi 1982, pp. 13–14).

The story of resistance and collaboration, as portrayed by Ngugi, has a certain unity of view which lacks precision when one is searching for a complex interpretation of history. First, this approach tends to oversimplify the real nature of the colonial and imperialist context within which the initiatives of resistance and collaboration by Africans were undertaken. The impression Ngugi creates is that the choice between collaboration and resistance was always a simple one in which the loyalists were always motivated by sheer economic greed, while the resisters were motivated by their love for humanity. Second, Ngugi gives the impression that once one was in the loyalists' camp one remained there and ensured that one's progeny continued to prosper. There are no grey areas in Ngugi's colonial and postcolonial worlds. One is either a patriot or a traitor. But, as Berman and Lonsdale argue:

> The development and character of the African *petit-bourgeoisie* in Kenya, and elsewhere in colonial Africa, cannot be understood outside its deeply ambivalent relationship with the colonial state. This ambivalence, expressed in sharply contrasting and often alternating patterns of collaboration and conflict, encouragement and constraint, attraction and rejection, was felt both by African and the colonial authorities and was grounded in some of the most fundamental contradictions of colonialism. (1992a, p. 197)

Evidently, the dialectic of collaboration and struggle which characterised the relationship between the emergent African *petit-bourgeoisie* and the colonial state was a complex one in which grounds were ever shifting, positions were never permanent and relationships were never free of conflict and contradictions. For example, Marshall Clough (1990) has demonstrated that the position of the African chiefs, particularly in the Kiambu district of Kenya, kept on shifting, depending on whether or not their interests and those of their subjects were threatened. Paradoxically, Kiambu, which was regarded by the colonial officials as a soft and loyal district, was also the home area of such key political leaders as Harry Thuku, Koinange wa Mbiyu and Jomo Kenyatta. It is also the district that lost most land to settlers in spite of protests (Clough 1990, pp. 65–7).

William Ochien'g has also questioned the popular assumption that all loyalists were motivated by personal economic greed. He writes that the so-called Mau Mau loyalists were neither stooges nor self-seekers but an integral part of the struggle of Africans for progress and dignity in the face of acute political and economic difficulties (Ochien'g 1972, pp. 46–70). Ochien'g's position is also supported by M. Tarmakin, who sees the Mau Mau loyalists 'as having entered in the political struggle to defend legitimate group interests, to promote their political ideals and even to fight for what they regarded as the interests of their fellow Africans' (1978, pp. 247–61).[5] The loyalists, for example, saw themselves as the legitimate defenders of progress and development, which were best expressed in Christianity, education and investment in small business and farming.[6] They were defending a way of life. In other words, for the loyalists colonial policy could be contested within limits, the bounds of which were often violated by the young rebels who, in their view, had no reverence for the Kikuyu traditions of respect for elders and were threatening the community. Therefore, the relationship between the loyalists and the colonial state was never a linear one. Ironically, the moral complexity of the Mau Mau, as I have argued, was well captured in Ngugi's early novels, particularly, *Weep Not, Child* and *A Grain of Wheat*.

Ngugi's portrayal of workers and the emergent African *petit-bourgeoisie* robs them of initiative in the context of decolonisation. The workers and peasants are doomed to a vicious circle of poverty which renders all their struggles irrelevant because there are no gains – no democratic scores in the postcolonial state after many years of anticolonial struggle. They cannot manipulate spaces open to them and, when they try to do so, like Wanja in *Petals of Blood*, all efforts are brought to naught by big capital. The native bourgeoisie, on the other hand, are mere 'watchdogs' of foreign capital. They are not innovative, but are instead reckless imitators of Western values – the masters that they serve dutifully. The Kenyan *petit-bourgeoisie* are portrayed as having no desire to be their own masters, but wanting simply to limp after the image of the Western bourgeoisie. Those who want to be their own masters like Mwereri wa Mukiraai are eliminated.

Dependency Theory and Class Dynamics

The picture of the national bourgeoisie as mere puppets or watchdogs of the white imperialists, and as totally powerless without their masters, is hard to sustain and it tends to over-simplify a rather complex class dynamic in Africa. The problem is inherent in dependency theory in that it tends to divert attention from the national struggles within Africa by 'underplaying the growth of real local divisions' (Cooper 1992, p. 38), and by implying that the local bourgeoisie may not be as dangerous as the international capital that it serves. Dependency theory seeks to explain the problems of Africa, and indeed those of the so-called 'Third World', as problems of global imperialism 'depicted as part of a self-reproducing global system in which the perverse underdevelopment of the periphery was the necessary mirror of genuine capitalist development at the centre' (Berman and Lonsdale 1992a, p. 197).

Ngugi is a prisoner of the broad perspective of dependency theory. In most of his works, he creates a simplistic binary opposition between the oppressor and the oppressed, which precludes any possibility of conflicting interests within these broad social categories. Apart from conflating workers and peasants into one group, without any social content or specific defining features, Ngugi's construction of 'the people' in these broad categories of the leaders and the led, the oppressor and the oppressed, constitutes 'the people' as lacking initiative – a passive group which is acted upon.[7] And although Ngugi attempts to create a picture of an heroic collective of workers and peasants, they come through as faceless. The so-called power of the working people is not visible beyond the slogans of the workers, undefined strikes and mass demonstrations (Ngugi 1977, p. 4). The workers do not seem to have any visible conflicts of interest other than the politics of ethnic divisiveness which Ngugi presents as primarily a construction of the elite. Wanja seems to be speaking for Ngugi when she insinuates that it is the rich – 'the Mercedes family' – who are preoccupied with cultivating ethnic divisions to delude the workers into believing that there is no divide between the rich and the poor within one ethnic community.

> For to us what did it matter who drove a Mercedes Benz? They were all one tribe; the Mercedes family: whether they came from the coast or from Kisumu. One family. We were another tribe: another family. (Ngugi 1977, p. 98)

Ngugi tends to dismiss ethnicity as an invention of colonialism and the ruling elite in Kenya. The likes of Moi and his cohort group, according to this logic, are therefore responsible for generating ethnic consciousness and manipulating, to their advantage, what was invented by the colonialists.

Ngugi's argument that modern ethnicity is a product of colonial history of divide-and-rule, which helped to give the 'tribe' its real identity by 'specifying "tribes" culturally within the context of a uniquely colonial sociology', to use Vail's words, may have some strength (Vail 1989, p. 3). His pet argument, that ethnicity is an ideological mask employed by ambitious and crafty members of the *petit-bourgeoisie* as a way of securing their own interests against the ever-growing class divisions within their own ethnic groups, may also have certain elements of truth in it. However, Ngugi's dual stance, while having some validity, does not answer the question why ethnic consciousness and its close relative, regionalism, remain attractive to ordinary Kenyans long after the colonial period. Why was it possible to revitalise ethnicity so easily and to mobilise popular opinion around ethnicity, for example, in the recent multiparty elections in Kenya?[8]

The position taken in this book is that 'ethnicity is not a natural cultural residue but a consciously crafted ideological creation' (Vail 1989, p. 7). The construction of ethnicity, however, is not always from above. Quite often it is also given impetus by practical needs of those from below and the actual persistence of 'ethnic moments of identity' (Piper *et al.* 1992, p. 13). The theory that the African masses are gullible pawns – easily manipulated by colonialists and the crafty African elite into ethnic consciousness – is ripe for debunking. Ethnicity, when seen as a mechanism for political and economic control, ceases to be the often abhorred return to primordial values, or a monopoly of the ruling elite in which they manipulate the ignorant masses in the struggle for power in the modern state.

Ethnicity, on the contrary, should be seen as an important instrument of control steeped in ethnic ideologies and in group interests that are constantly changing. In the words of Berman and Lonsdale, ethnicity is 'a vehicle of unquestioning sectional ambition' (1992b, p. 317). In this struggle to realise sectarian ambitions, ordinary people have found ethnicity useful in protecting internal rights and as a defence against external threats, whether real or perceived. Of course, in the invention of ethnicity and its appropriation into competitive politics, the elite have emerged as the most eloquent articulators of the cultural characteristics of their ethnic identities through written histories, accounts of traditional ways of the tribe, and through written ethnic literatures.

In this sense, it might be argued that even Ngugi has, in modern Kenya, contributed to the reinvention of Agikuyu ethnic consciousness by resorting to the use of Gikuyu in his recent creative works and essays.[9] But, ultimately, it is competitive politics and the fear of economic exclusion that have made ethnicity, with its appeal to common heritage of the group and its land, so attractive in modern times. As Gerhard Mare has observed, material (and ultimately political) factors provide the impetus for ethnic moments of identity to be transformed into politicised ethnicity:

> Political ethnicity (ethnic nationalism) moves social identity to political agency, provides the means for political mobilisation, and submits the ethnic identity and group to another set of rules – those of competition for power. (1992, p. 43)

Evidently, if Mare's argument carries some weight, then ethnicity cannot be dismissed as an invention of colonialism and the intellectual elite in Africa, as scholars like Ngugi are wont to do. Neither is it useful to dismiss ethnicity as false consciousness. It is, in my view, an effective instrument in a political power game in which the ordinary people are as much active agents as the ruling elite in Africa. There is 'nothing wicked', to use Lonsdale's phrase, in ethnicity's 'modern persistence' (Berman and Lonsdale 1992b, p. 329). Instead, in a society such as Kenya, which is still groping for a sense of nationhood, and, indeed, striving to build a modern state, one should expect a coexistence of multiple identities, often in a continuous and dynamic tension. The Mau Mau songs, for example, were used by ordinary men and women to express their identity both as belonging to the house of Mumbi (meaning the Agikuyu community) and also with the desire for the broader Kenyan nationhood in the face of colonial oppression. Here was a classic case of two layers of identity coexisting within the consciousness of a specific ethnic community in Kenya. The construction of a specifically Agikuyu identity did not preclude the imagination of the wider Kenyan identity.

Lastly, Ngugi's narrative seems to be silent on the role of dissenting voices within the church. His presentation of religion is one-dimensional. For Ngugi, religion is a tool of oppression; a vehicle for lulling the poor and turning them away from the material reality of this world. No one doubts that religion in Kenya has in certain instances served to entrench and justify exploitation in both colonial and post-colonial contexts. But it is doubtful that religious groups are mute tools of exploitation, as past and recent histories of such groups have proved in Kenya.[10] At the height of intertribal (ethnic) tension in 1969, when a section of the Agikuyu took to oathing, which Ngugi refers to as the 'tea party' (Ngugi 1977, p. 84), it was the National Christian Council of Kenya (NCCK) that condemned its ethnic parochialism.[11] In the run-up to multiparty elections in 1992, the church (under the NCCK umbrella) played a crucial role in calling on the government to democratise the levers of governance and appealed to the opposition to forge unity in the interest of the nation. A leading Kenyan weekly wrote:

After leading the way for the opposition, the NCCK was now shepherding the opposition itself. Indeed the NCCK and some of the opposition figures have fought parallel battles against the government in the past six years. Some

of the clerics ... have, over the years tended to be more
critical of the government than many of the radical
politicians. (*The Weekly Review*, 19 June 1992, p. 4)

Ngugi's classical understanding of religion cannot allow him
to appreciate the role played by the church in contemporary
politics. More importantly, he fails to accept the church as an
enduring form of popular organisation in which 'the people'
take the initiative in interpreting and integrating their world
so as to gain some control over it. A complex reading of
religion should see it as a vehicle for cognition; as the space
for relating the self to the material and the spiritual being.

In conclusion, it seems fair to argue that the weaknesses
inherent in Ngugi's sense of history in the later texts are in
fact attributable in a large measure to the weaknesses of
dependency perspective, which are manifested in the
suppression of specific and local conflicts and the privileging
of the centre–periphery approach.[12] Thus, a single-track
theory which seeks to explain Kenya's underdevelopment
only in terms of the centre as a block exploiting the periphery
fails to grasp the specific character of capitalist development
in Kenya and, subsequently, to lay down proper political
strategies for meaningful change. The point to reiterate is that
Ngugi's ideological framework, underpinned by Fanon's conceptualisation of the 'African revolution' and dependency
perspective, tends to obscure the way in which classes
reproduce themselves and derive any relative autonomy of
politics in the class formations. It therefore obscures the par-
ticularities of different social formations. Ngugi is clearly
imprisoned within a static evaluation of classes and his
framework tends to be rigidly deterministic in locating
connections between the state and capital, in depicting the
national bourgeoisie as mere puppets or watchdogs of
Western capital, and in insisting that there is continuity
between resistance in the colonial state and resistance in the
postcolonial state. Indeed, evaluation is deterministic in its
espousal of a linear reproduction of the colonial class
formations into the postcolonial state.

The path to meaningful social change in Africa cannot
ignore the internal contradictions and the specific social

dynamics of the postcolonial state. And yet the fundamental precondition for democratic transformation is that unrelenting struggle to create space for political dialogue and change. In this act of social transformation Ngugi has played his part precisely because his narrative discourse, whatever its limitations, 'is dominated by its transformative "text" in which the captive nation, overcome in recent history, awaits its desired redemption' (Gurnah 1993, p. 142).

2

The Changing Nature of Allegory in Ngugi's Novels

Recent studies on postcolonial theories have attempted to redeem the notion of allegory from its traditional conception as 'a constrained and mechanical mode of expression' (Slemon 1988, p. 157). Allegory, they argue, has been reappropriated by the postcolonial writers as a strategy against the reconstruction of the colonised by the coloniser. It is a reappropriation because allegory, in their view, 'historically meant a way of speaking for the subjugated others of the European colonial enterprise – a way of subordinating the colonised through the politics of representation' (Slemon 1987, p. 8). It is because these theories challenge the monolithic representation of the colonised that allegory has been transformed into 'a site upon which post-colonial cultures seek to contest and subvert colonialist appropriation through the production of a literary, and specifically anti-imperialist, figurative opposition or textual counter-discourse' (p. 10). Postcolonial allegory thus acquires a transformative capacity in its attempt to subvert or challenge the imperial myths and codes that make up the colonised peoples' notions of received history. Allegory, Slemon adds:

> provides the post-colonial writer with a means of fore-grounding such inherited notions and exposing them to the transformative powers of imagination; and in doing so, post-colonial allegory helps to produce new ways of seeing history, new ways of 'reading' the world. (1988, p. 164)

As suggested in the previous chapter and in the introduction, Ngugi's texts fall under the rubric of counter-narratives to colonial history. It seems to me that Ngugi, in trying to fulfil the demands of an historical novel and the demands of

44

rewriting and giving alternative interpretation of Kenyan history, has tended to fall back on the allegorical mode and popular forms in his representation (see Chapter 4).

Taken from the Greek word 'allos', allegory means the other, that is, in saying one thing you also imply something else. It is writing that involves, as Stephen Slemon puts it, 'doubling or reduplicating extra-textual material; and since the allegorical sign refers always to a previous or anterior sign' it will always draw our attention to the passage of time; it will inevitably create an awareness of the past – a conscious-ness of history and tradition (1988, p. 158). This has frequently led to the drawing of links between allegory and history. Allegorical writing, it is argued, concerns itself primarily with 'redeeming or recuperating the past, either because the present pales in comparison with it, or because the past has become in some ways unacceptable to the dominant ideology of contemporary society' (p. 158). The allegorical text, it would seem from this argument, is bound to the authority of the past and is often deployed in the service of ordering historical narratives.

Walter Benjamin, in his study of *Trauerspiel*, has added some illuminating dimensions to the theoretical assumption that allegory is a popular mode for recuperating the past and ordering history. According to Benjamin, in periods of frag-mentation and displacement, allegory is often the mode best suited for piecing history together. This is because allegory's tendency towards a linear typology would provide the writer, in a situation of fragmentation and marginality, with a coherent framework within which to rewrite history (Benjamin 1977).

It is not difficult to see why Ngugi resorts to allegory in his narratives. Ngugi grew under the shadow of colonialism and was directly affected by it. His brother was killed in the Mau Mau war and as a young man he worked in the settler farms because his own parents had no land: 'My father and his four wives had no land. They lived as tenants-at-will on somebody else's land' (Ngugi 1972, p. 48). Ngugi is a product of a settler colony in which land alienation, dispossession of people, and disruption of precolonial (read 'traditional') modes of production became the central point in the nationalist politics in Kenya. And in more recent times, Ngugi, as a writer of praxis whose freedom of expression has constantly been suppressed by successive postcolonial regimes, is always dogged by conditions of fragmentation. Indeed, he was detained for his writing by the authorities. Significantly, his most obvious example of allegorical narrative, *Devil on the Cross*, was written in prison. Like Bunyan writing *The Pilgrim's Progress* in Bedford gaol, Ngugi wrote *Devil on the Cross* in Kamiti Maximum Security Prison in Kenya. Again, given prison conditions – without proper writing material and in isolation from the rest of society – Ngugi wrote out of exile; he wrote from a situation of displacement and fragmentation.[1] Ngugi's recourse to allegory would seem to be a strategy aimed at creating some sense out of a state of chaos; a way of reclaiming Kenya's history, once suppressed in the colonial state and again in the postcolonial state. Allegorical writing, for Ngugi, must have opened up the possibility of transformation – a means of rereading the imperial myths and their social agents in the postcolonial state.

Allegory in Ngugi's Earlier Texts

Ngugi's return to the past is a common feature in his narrative. The past is often evoked by Ngugi as a challenge and at times a parallel to the present state of chaos. Where colonialism denied histories and traditions, Ngugi seeks to found a sense of self in a recovery of history, a recuperation of tradition. This impulse to re-establish the vital link with the past, Gikandi writes of East African novels, is underpinned by the powerful evocation of land: 'the vital link between man and nature ... the principal means of production whose loss signifies the disruptive and savage nature of imperial conquest' (Gikandi 1984, p. 235).

Ngugi's earlier texts bear that powerful evocation of land, both as a signifier of a glorious past in which man and woman were in harmony with nature and thereby presupposing a stable identity associated with landownership, and land as a signifier of loss whose recovery would imply the recovery of identity. The rooting of national identity in Agikuyu mythology, as I have argued in the last chapter, highlights the tensions between constructions of ethnic tradition and the building of a modern nation-state. Ngugi uses allegory to negotiate this tension and to suggest that if in the past national identity was inscribed in the land designated by the founders of the community, colonialism, in usurping the land, disrupts this identity. Thus the myth of creation which legitimises the claim to landownership by turning it into a covenant between man and his creators transforms this land into an inviolable and living entity; it transforms land into a space for cultural and political contestation.

Nothing captures this flux better than the way the two ridges and the valley of life are personified in *The River Between*. Ngugi's restoration project is 'embodied by the land, the novel's larger-than-life character, which provides not only the physical context within which the lives of the other characters can be worked out, but also a force they can identify with' (Gikandi 1984, p. 237). The people's past before the ravages of colonialism is typified in Honia river, with its healing powers. The river which united the people now divides them under colonialism.

It is the land loss, occasioned by colonialism, that *Weep Not, Child* explores. Ngotho, the patriarch of African heritage and tradition, treats land with reverence and he is profoundly alienated by the ensuing issues engendered by its loss. After all, land provides the spiritual link to his ancestors: 'He owed it to the dead, the living and the unborn of his line, to keep guard over it' (Ngugi 1964, p. 31). This same land is viewed by the colonial settler, Mr Howlands, as virgin and wild, only fit to be conquered and tamed. For Mr Howlands Kenya 'was a big trace of wild country to conquer'(p. 30) and '[h]e alone was responsible for taming this unoccupied wildness' (p. 31).

Evidently, land, as the central metaphor in Ngugi's texts, serves a metonymic function, figuring the glorious past of the community, now in ruins, and a past whose restoration is only possible through land restitution. The most striking anxiety of the people in Ngugi's texts is land alienation. The Kiama rejects Waiyaki because he cannot speak to the land agenda, which as I have noted in the previous chapter, is mystically associated with the purity of the community and its genesis. Boro's disenchantment with the elders and his father in particular is because they cannot fight for the restoration of the land. It is the same anxiety for land restoration that pervades *A Grain of Wheat* on the eve of independence: 'Would Uhuru bring land into African hands?' Gikonyo asks (Ngugi 1967, p. 208). And yet, in spite of the strong sense of loss, there is also a strong sense of retrieval paralleled by the desire for land restoration. And here land not only means the physical space, but more significantly it signifies the nation. As a physical space, Ngugi embraces the rural topology as the signifier of genuine nationalism. The urban area is associated with modern degradation. The youthful radicals get their ideas from the city and they would seem to have lost their humanity. The city, in *A Grain of Wheat*, stands as an aberration, remote and away from the peasants of Thabai. It is the city that hoards Uhuru from the people. Nairobi is a place where post-independence politicians disappear and meet with foreigners. The image of the city as alienating, in the Marxian sense, continues to haunt Ngugi's later novels. However, to express his desire for 'genuine' nationalism, Ngugi conflates both allegory and symbolism: land stands for nationhood rooted in the people's values while at the same time allegorising the state of the nation – 'a nation in turmoil' as Kihika refers to it (Ngugi 1967, p. 15). It is the allegorical redemption of the nation under colonial ruins that is embodied in the Moses figure, the allegorical redeemer, that seems to cut across all works of Ngugi. Ngugi's allegory is therefore rooted in a certain type of nationalism that seeks to fabricate a discourse of resistance and liberation. Liberation and the reclaiming of history go hand in hand, and are explored in a range of ways.

Ngugi's nationalism works through an allegorical typology of characters in which the coloniser is invariably portrayed in grotesque images while the colonised is given normal and realistic characterisation. The coloniser tends to be unnatural while the colonised African is natural. Ngugi thus engages in a reversal of the manichean structure which, JanMohamed (1983) argues, following Fanon, characterises colonial societies and rests on a racial allegory. Mr Howlands in *Weep*

Not, Child is not very different from Dr Henry Van Dyke in *A Grain of Wheat*. They both have a sagging stomach that becomes the predominant figure of exploitation and deflated power in Ngugi's later novels. The pot-belly signifies the depraved picture of the *petit-bourgeoisie* in the postcolonial state that Ngugi uses to laugh at power and authority in *Devil on the Cross*. Mr Howlands is described as 'a typical settler' – the man 'with an oval-shaped face that ended in double chin and a big stomach' (Ngugi 1964, p. 30). He is the exact opposite of Ngotho who is portrayed with depth and complexity. Ngotho's affinity to land is portrayed as natural while Mr Howland's smacks of an obsession, a disease in the psyche of the colonial settler, to conquer land as a release from a nervous condition and therefore irrational. This association between insanity and land, irrationality and violence, is, however, not confined to whites. When Boro abandons the primary objective of land restitution in pursuit of personal revenge, he can only degenerate into reckless violence hitherto associated with the coloniser only. The settler figure is, however, the stark antithesis of the colonised. The settlers are associated with degenerate values, often unfaithful in their marriages and leading hollow lives like that of the Thompsons in *A Grain of Wheat*. The weaknesses are specifically expressed in loose sexual behaviour and drunkenness among the settler community.

Ngugi seems to intimate that personal narratives of the settler community, characterised by moral degeneration and frustrated life histories, allegorises the crisis of the Empire as sick and decaying from within. It is an empire in search of moral authority. This is contrasted by the ideal African authority embodied in the patriarch figure, Ngotho. What marks Ngotho's household is peace and stability and the family only breaks down due to colonial onslaught. Ngotho's household, accordingly, allegorises a glorious African past threatened by a colonial regime presided over by schizophrenic power brokers under whose authority the African society can only disintegrate. The allegorical typology employed by Ngugi here is both constraining and romantic when it comes to the ideal African symbol and exaggerated with reference to colonial figures, almost giving us ahistorical structures. And yet one of the primary functions of allegory is to constrain the ability of the reader to construct meaning because allegory is, by definition, 'a sign that refers to one meaning and thus exhausts its suggestive potentialities once it has been deciphered' (de Man 1983, p. 188). Ngugi seeks to turn the manichean principle of racial allegory on its head in order to restore full humanity to the African. He sets out to challenge, in a subtle way, the notes for a philosophical book entitled *Prospero in Africa*, which Mr Thompson intends to write – a book in which '*primordial trees have always awed primitive minds*' (Ngugi 1964, p. 55). Whether Ngugi is talking here about what Said calls 'idyllic meadows' (1994, p. 253) seems to be irrelevant. He is locating his discourse on a certain type of nationalism that is rooted in a reversal of binary codes of imperialism and this in itself is an important process in reconstituting a shattered community.

One of the ways in which Ngugi achieves his anti-imperialist nationalism is to give a voice to hitherto repressed voices of the colonial subject and to compress the coloniser's voice into some isolated figures within a sociopolitical landscape saturated by the native. In the *The River Between* the conflict is essentially about creating a new mythos for the community and at the heart of this struggle it is the privileged voice of the Africans, with their tensions and contradictions, that is heard. As one of the more influential thinkers of Kenyan nationalism, Ngugi responds to the problems of using history in the reconstruction of national identity through modes that highlight the tensions between the constructions of tradition and the implicit modernity of the nascent Kenyan nation. Kabonyi and the Kiama represent a specific strand of nationalism rooted purely in a static tradition that Ngugi seeks to transcend. Waiyaki, on the other hand, while accepting that identity is imperative, insists that it is not enough to assert a different identity. One has to accept the fact that he or she is part of an historical process that is dynamic and one which opens up the possibilities for development and growth. Waiyaki becomes the new symbol of hybridity caught in between a tumultuous historical process whose course he seeks to influence. Thus the allegorising of historical consciousness as nationalist finds its ultimate expression in the figure of Waiyaki. He heralds the kind of consciousness, albeit more radical, that Matigari embodies in the postcolonial Kenyan state. Later, in *A Grain of Wheat* and in the subsequent novels, Ngugi seeks to further problematise the nationalist consciousness found in *The River Between* through an allegorical character typology of patriots and traitors. This time Ngugi injects a basic class conscious-ness in his narrative and suggests that the construction of the Kenyan nation ought to be much more complex and more discriminating than his previous discourses had implied. If the previous discourses were premised on an anticolonial agenda and unity of the colonised, now Ngugi argues for a transcendence of undifferentiated community. It is this con-sciousness that Kihika embodies: "'A day comes when brother shall give up brother, a mother her son, when you and I have heard the call of a nation in turmoil'" (Ngugi 1967, p. 15).

The rejection of unity based on kinship bonds is at the heart of Kihika's statement. His consciousness eludes the alienated Mugo and sets him apart from Karanja, the colonial surrogate whose figure redefines the new relationships in the colonial world. These characters now begin to reveal the specific political unconscious behind their lives. The political unconscious referred to here transcends the manichean allegory of race because it reconfigures the colonised subject as constituted through multiple identities and a range of ideological matrices. The 'tribal mythos', which used to bind all the Agikuyu, would seem to collapse in the face of those forces of change and the new societal structures set in motion by colonialism. For example, the homeguard figure, embodied in the character of Karanja, is a product of colonialism. Karanja is following in the footsteps of Joshua and Jacobo before him, except now Ngugi is under no illusion that there remains any possibility of crossing the divide separating the traitors and patriots. Karanja in his position as a collaborator allegorises a new consciousness, based on self-interest as opposed to communal ethos, emerging out of the womb of colonial and capitalist ideology. Ngugi is by no means suggesting that the precolonial society was free of personal pursuits at the expense of the society, but rather that colonialism and the advent of capitalism exacerbated these values. He seems to intimate that the real anti-imperialist struggle was stunted by the betrayal and the subsequent hanging of Kihika – the symbol of revolutionary values in the novel. What now threatens Kenya's freedom, which Kihika symbolises, is rooted in this new consciousness that gestures towards neocolonialism. In other words, the web of betrayals that we encounter in the text are allegorical of betrayals in the post-independence period – a warning to readers of the possibility of disillusionment with Uhuru. The irony and facade that surrounds Mugo's heroism, the ineptitude and arrogance of the MP of Thabai and Gikonyo's narrow preoc-cupation with new capitalist enterprise, all point to 'an allegory of the embattled' nation, to use Jameson's phrase (1991, p. 86). This marks a definite shift away from the traditional colonial model to a consciousness informed by the capitalist perspective that is the target of Ngugi's critique in his later novels. As the colonialists recede in the background, a new class consisting of the nationalist fighters and the former homeguards emerges to the bewilderment of the common men and women of Thabai. For them the future holds no hope with the advent of new power relations of 'the local pro-foreigner *comprador* class' (Ngugi 1981b, p. 31). It is the ideological poverty of this new class that Ngugi caricatures in his later novels through the grotesque images of the body, while at the same time drawing attention to how the old social relations are reproduced in the present; how colonial relations of production reproduce themselves.

Allegory and Postcolonial Power Relations

As I have pointed out, Ngugi's return to the past is one of the constant allegorical markers in his narrative. Ngugi's stubborn return to the Mau Mau war and his constant use of the Mau Mau as a symbol of inspiration is a good example. A number of Ngugi's themes also find their thematic antecedents and parallels in the past of his characters. To do this Ngugi explores a specific time scheme in which the narrative swings from the past time of the action to the current time of the telling or retelling. In each of the two time zones the experiences of the action are not just lived and relived, but the narrative experiences of the past are in themselves a parallel and a commentary on the present situation. In his narration of the colonial past, for example, reside certain echoes of the postcolonial experiences in Kenya: narrative meaning in the colonial context allegorises narrative meaning in the postcolonial state. The two different time frames (then/now; now/then) are connected by some kind of development within 'continuity' and change within 'permanence'. Thus Ngugi's use of allegory would seem to point both to continuity and permanence, a situation in which, for example, the colonial configuration parallels the postcolonial state. The colonial condition would seem to reproduce itself in a linear fashion and the allegorical mode works to highlight this relationship.

A good example is Abdulla in *Petals of Blood*, a character who emerges as the reincarnation of Kenya's colonial past. He is a Mau Mau veteran who has nothing else to show for the sacrifices made during the struggle for independence but his stumped leg. Abdulla, through his reminiscences on the colonial struggle, gives us a perspective on Kenya's colonial past. But Abdulla's story is also presented as parallel to, and a mockery of, the present postcolonial state which is but a replica of the colonial past. Ordinarily, Abdulla's name means servant of Allah. But his real name is Murira (Ngugi 1977, pp. 61, 910), meaning 'the one who protects'. Having been a forest fighter, he is the reincarnation of the spirit of Kimathi. He is representative of the sacrifices made during the struggle of which the stump of his leg is a physical reminder. Abdulla links us with Kenya's past and preserves the memories of the unsung heroes of Kenya's freedom. He is one of the many heroes of Kenya's freedom struggle constantly evoked by Ngugi – heroes who have gained nothing from independence. His survival now is a matter of a painful self-reliance in the store and bar from which he ekes out a living. Like Wanja, he is portrayed as a victim of what Ngugi calls the neocolonialist forces of exploitation. It is these same forces of the postcolonial state which order the closure of Abdulla's 'dirty premises' to make way for the Trans-Africa road and Kimeria's business houses. In the end, Abdulla is totally impoverished. He turns into a tramp and a drunk, obsessed with revenge on

Kimeria who betrayed him to the colonialists and who continues to hound him in the postcolonial state.

In Abdulla's character Ngugi captures the enigmatic allegorical time frames in which the past confronts the present. Allegory here works through narrative duration, a process through which distance is created between sign and referent, past and present. What Ngugi creates is a philosophical irony in which the past stands in judgement over the present. Abdulla's life parallels that of Matigari, the hero of *Matigari*, written ten years later. Himself a former freedom fighter, Matigari is forced into a second war of liberation because not much has changed in favour of the oppressed majority in the postcolonial state. Like Abdulla, he adopts the young boy Muriuki who is symbolically poised to continue with the struggle after his death. Again like Abdulla who takes Wanja in the end, Matigari also takes Guthera, the abused woman, into his custody. Matigari is a continuation of Ngugi's figure of authority, the patriarch who protects both youth and womanhood.

Ngugi seems to be saying that if colonialism led to degradation of black life and exploitation of the marginalised groups in Kenya, then these forms of human degradation repeat themselves in the postcolonial state, except with the minor difference that in the colonial context the exploiters were white, aided by black zombies, while now exploiters are black working with their masters in Europe. For example, Karega fought against a white headmaster at Siriana high school and had him replaced by a black headmaster, Mr Chui. Soon Karega and his schoolmates discover that Chui was no different from the white headmaster he replaced. In the postcolonial struggle against the owners of Theng'eta Breweries in Ilmorog, Karega, as a trade union leader, is confronted by the same Chui in partnership with foreign capital. Thus, in Ngugi's narrative discourse, the past is clearly parallel with the present at all levels of society: educational, cultural, economic and even personal. Wanja and Wariinga, in *Petals of Blood* and *Devil on the Cross* respectively, are both victims of bad educational leadership and a system in which children are exposed to violent and sexual abuse by educators. They are also victims of economic deprivation which leaves them vulnerable to sexual exploitation by the rich. Wanja's and Wariinga's present lives are but a repeat performance of their past experiences. The past, whether public or private, continues to repeat itself; the past remains an allegorical reflection of the present. The emergent nationalists whose greed had become apparent on the eve of independence now flaunt their power in disgrace and openly. It is the absurdity of their mimicry of the former colonial masters and the turning of a postcolony into a theatre stage within which power is performed that Ngugi caricatures in his later novels, through the grotesque image of the body. What follows is an attempt to place Ngugi's use of the grotesque within the basic concerns of the novel *Devil on the Cross*, where the features are most glaring.

Allegorical Satire and the Grotesque Image of the Body

Achille Mbembe, in a paper entitled 'Provisional Notes on the Postcolony', draws our attention to the nature of power and its actual performance in a postcolony. He characterises a postcolony simply as those societies which have recently emerged from the experience of colonisation and exhibit the violence which the colonial relationship *par excellence* involves. He argues that the 'post-colony is characterised by a distinctive style of political improvisation, by a tendency to excess and a lack of proportion ... [and] ... a series of corporate institutions and political machinery which, once they are in place, constitute a distinctive regime of violence' (Mbembe 1992, p. 3). The postcolony in fact becomes some form of stage on which 'the wider problems and its corollary discipline' are played out (p. 3). It is this theatrical display of power that Mbembe calls the banality of power in the postcolony. He uses banality to mean 'those elements of the obscene and the grotesque that Mikhail Bakhtin claims to have located in 'non-official' cultures but which, in fact, are intrinsic to all systems of domination and to the means by which those systems are confirmed or deconstructed' (p. 3). Thus the grotesque and the obscene would seem to be some of the basic characteristics that identify postcolonial regimes of domination.

The writing of Ngugi's *Devil on the Cross* was in more than one sense a product of the postcolonial violence to which Mbembe draws our attention. It was written while Ngugi was in detention. It marked the actual enactment of violence in a postcolony through the capture and isolation of the body under the guise of the Public Security Order inherited from the colonial regime. In *Detained*, Ngugi confesses that the novel was written 'with blood, sweat and toil' (1981a, p. 3). Having failed to control Ngugi, the Kenyatta regime sends him to solitary confinement which is, as Michel Foucault reminds us, 'certainly the most frenzied manifestation of power imaginable' (1984, p. 210). In writing this novel, Ngugi seems to have refused to succumb to the dictates of violence to which the Kenyan regime often resorts in silencing all its critics. The novel became Ngugi's weapon for preserving the body and for overcoming the state of fragmentation imposed by the regime. Wariinga, the heroine of toil and the harbinger of freedom, whose image looms large in the text, was conceived in cell 16 in 1978 (Ngugi 1981a, p. 3). If the regime's aim was to break Ngugi and to reconfigure his body, in *Devil on the Cross*, he turns this attempt upside down. Instead, it is to the obscene body of the postcolonial regime weighed down by its 'impotence', that Ngugi directs our laughter. But, first, the content of *Devil on the Cross*.

The novel deals with a group of six protagonists travelling together in a *matatu* taxi to Ilmorog. The protagonists discover that they are all mysteriously invited to a Devil's feast, where thieves and robbers of Kenya enter a competition for the election of the seven cleverest thieves and robbers. The characters are Wariinga, Wangari, Gatuiria, Muturi, Mwireri and Mwaura the driver. The narrative operates at two levels: the allegorical story illustrated by the competition or feast organised by the Devil, and the story of Wariinga who is the pivot of the plot. Like *Petals of Blood*, the novel takes place mainly in Ilmorog and partly in Nairobi. The novel is dedicated to 'all Kenyans struggling against the neo-colonial stage of imperialism' (Ngugi 1987, p. 5). It is no wonder, then, that the major trope in *Devil on the Cross* should be neocolonial dependency, with the Devil on the cross as the structuring symbol. This is best illustrated in Wariinga's nightmare in which the white colonialist Devil is crucified by the masses, apparent reference to political independence, only to be rescued by the local comprador. Significantly, 'The Devil had two mouths, one on his forehead and the other at the back of his head. His belly sagged, as if it were about to give birth to all the evils of the world. His skin was red, like that of a pig' (p. 13). This is significant because the physical features of the Devil draw attention to his grotesque image, the same image that he gives to those that rescue him and in turn serve him. Significantly, again, the Devil rewards his rescuers by fattening their bellies. It turns out that a 'Devil's feast' is arranged by the local 'thieves' to commemorate a visit by foreign guests – 'particularly from America, England, Germany, France, Italy, Sweden and Japan' – as part of 'the International Organisation of Thieves and Robbers' (p. 78).

The creation of a Devil's feast, where national robbers and their foreign allies gather in order to reveal their tactics and motives, provides Ngugi with the space for erecting or deconstructing, through the grotesque and the obscene, the banality of power in a postcolony. Ngugi uses the Bakhtinian notion of the grotesque and obscenity by turning the rulers of postcolony into objects of ridicule and in the process transcends the limitations Bakhtin imposes on the two terms by suggesting that the grotesque and the obscene are not simply confined to the province of the ruled, but could be extended to the rulers. It is to the local comprador bourgeoisie, who boast about their cleverness and their cunning on how to steal from the people as well as how to bow to foreign control, that the grotesque is restricted. He does this by exposing how state power – represented by the local comprador – dramatises its own magnificence through an absurd ceremonial display of their wealth as spectacles worthy of emulation by the ruled. It is in this feast that Ngugi erects the monstrous image of capitalism as a fetish. The worshippers of the fetish gather to preach before it, 'the fiction of its perfection' (Mbembe 1992, p. 21). Each and every speaker that takes the stage demonstrates, in blunt testimonies, that the postcolony has been turned into a stage for bizarre self-gratification; an absurd display of buffoons, fools and clowns in the feast of 'modern robbery and theft'.

The feast becomes the privileged language through which power speaks, acts and coerces. The speech by the leader of the foreign delegation of thieves and robbers, in which he arrogantly admonishes the local delegates 'to drink the blood of [their] people and to eat their flesh, [as the imperial powers have done to the Africans over the centuries], than to retreat a step' (Ngugi 1987, p. 89), signifies greed and power magnified to their full and logical extremes – reduced to their essences. Yet the actual idiom of this display, its organisation and its symbolism, focuses on the body: specifically the belly, the mouth and the phallus.

Ngugi's thieves display striking forms of deformity. His portrayal of the local thieves at the cave foregrounds the grotesque image of the body in which the belly and the mouth stand out. One striking example is that of Gitutu. Ngugi's satire on the comprador class, his laughter at their borrowed power, is best captured in the narrator's graphic description of Gitutu's body:

> Gitutu had a belly that protruded so far that it would have touched the ground had it not been supported by the braces that held up his trousers. It seemed as if his belly had absorbed all his limbs and all the other organs of his body. Gitutu had no neck – at least, his neck was not visible. His arms and legs were short stumps. His head had shrunk to the size of a fist. (Ngugi 1987, p. 99)

Gitutu's body is a body in the act of becoming; 'it is continually built, created, and builds and [it in turn] creates another body' (Bakhtin 1968, p. 317). It is a body that, figuratively speaking, swallows the world and is itself swallowed by the world. In the words of Bakhtin, the grotesque body 'outgrows its own self, transgressing its own body, in which it conceives a new, second body: the bowels and the phallus' (p. 317). In this act of swallowing, Gitutu's body becomes monstrous – a typical grotesque hyperbole. His belly threatens to detach itself from the body and lead an independent life. His neck, arms, legs and head have been transformed into a grotesque animal subject.

The realisation of the grotesque image of the body by associating the parts or the whole body with the animal form is best illustrated again in the body of Gitutu and, to a degree, in the body of Kihaahu, whose grotesque feature is his mouth rather than his stomach. To do this, Ngugi uses names which are semantically fixed to the master code of the Agikuyu people. The names are culturally positioned or grounded to a 'pretext' that is inherent in the tradition of the Gikuyu, and in particular to some animal or inanimate object in the Agikuyu cosmos whose traits the characters personify or share. For the average Agikuyu reader the names are specific signs which they could readily interpret because of the shared typology of meaning between the signs and their interpreters.

The name Gitutu wa Gataanguru is a good illustration of the use of this mutually intelligible typology of meaning between the sign and its community of readers. Gitutu in Gikuyu, Ndigirigi writes, refers to a 'big jigger', while Gataanguru refers to 'a belly infested with tapeworms which produce a bloating effect' (1991, p. 101). His physical form resembles that of a jigger. Thus Gitutu's name within the context of the Agikuyu readership helps to concretise the grotesque image of Gitutu's body. There are clear grounds for comparison in which the physical features of Gitutu – 'pot-belly', 'short-limbs' and 'tiny head' are placed in stark juxtaposition to the physical features of a jigger. But more importantly, these features underscore the parasitic nature of jiggers and by extension the parasitism of the ruling class in the postcolonial state that Gitutu represents or parallels. As a parasite, Gitutu finds his host in the lives of the workers and peasants that he exploits. Characteristic of this class, Ngugi seems to suggest, Gitutu eats more than he needs as he shamelessly confesses that his 'belly is becoming larger and larger because it is constantly overworked!' (Ngugi 1987, p. 100).

But, as if Gitutu's deformity is not a sufficient sign of the elites' greed, Ngugi's thieves seek true monstrosity, as in the case of Ndikita wa Nguunji who argues for additional human parts (Ngugi 1987, p. 180). Ndikita desires a world in which 'the rich few would ensure their immortality through the purchase of spare organs of the human body, thus leaving

death as the sole prerogative of the poor' (p. 100). Yet
Ndikita's desire to have spare organs serves to expose the
insecurity of masculine authority: for when Ndikita's wife
becomes enthusiastic about the prospect of having two female
organs, he is threatened. Ndikita expresses horror at the idea
of such equality between sexes and he urges his wife to
espouse, instead, 'true' African culture, to heed tradition,
which Ndikita would like to interpret as meaning inferior
status for women. As Eileen Julien writes: 'Ndikita would seem
to need women as witnesses of his masculine prowess, yet he
fears them and their sexual demands' (1992, pp. 149–50). It is
to serve his own masculine quest for privilege and power that
he invokes the authority of 'tradition'. Thus, the uncondi-
tional subordination of women to the principle of male
pleasure remains one of the pillars upholding the reproduction of the phallocratic system which turns postcoloniality
into 'a world of anxious virility, a world hostile to continence,
frugality, sobriety' (Mbembe 1992, p. 9). Wariinga's body, for
example, becomes the focus of a power struggle with far-
reaching ramifications. Masculine authority seeks to imprison
her body within the grip and grasp of the local thieves – the
ruling elite of the postcolonial state. But it is not until
Wariinga regains her agency as an active participant in the
process of history-making that she develops from the victim
type to the fighting type.

But it is not enough, in the postcolonial context, simply to
bring into play the mouth, the belly or phallus, or merely to
refer to them, in order to be automatically obscene. 'Mouth',
'belly', and 'phallus', when used in popular speech and jokes,
have above all to be located in the real world, located in real
time. In short, they are active statements about the human
condition, and as such contribute integrally to the making of
political culture in the postcolony. Every reference, then, to
mouth, belly or phallus is consequently a discourse on the
world – the postcolonial world. Ngugi's use of the grotesque
and the obscene points to this world.

Ngugi's use of the grotesque image of the body is very
much grounded in the ordinary politics of postcolonial
Kenya. It is the kind of politics whose primary objective is to
acquire power as the ultimate vehicle for economic success.

Most social struggles in Africa, Bayart is wont to remind us, only become useful if they lead to the accumulation of power: 'It is a truism that it is easier to get rich from a position of power than from a position of dependency and penury' (Bayart 1993, p. 239). When one acquires power and the economic success that goes with it, one becomes honoured and often one is not shy to perform one's success. Thus, in a postcolony, 'material prosperity is one of the chief political virtues rather than [the] object of disapproval' (Bayart 1993, p. 242). While writing *Devil on the Cross* Ngugi must have been conscious of the fact that boasting about one's wealth in Kenya is part of the social norm. As Angelique Haugerud reminds us: 'Exuberant showmanship is one enduring face of Kenyan political life' (1995, p. i). It is not unusual to come across politicians boasting about their wealth and with great admiration from the people. In the early days of Kenya's independence, Jomo Kenyatta – the first president of Kenya – ridiculed the radical nationalist opponent, Bildad Kaggia, for failing to amass wealth for himself. 'Look at Kungu Karumba,' Kenyatta told Kaggia, '[h]e has invested in buses and has earned money, but what have you done for yourself since independence?'[2] About two decades later, Mr Oloitiptip, one of President Moi's ministers, boasted to his political opponents in parliament in sentiments very similar to Kenyatta's when he declared: 'I've got money. I don't sell chickens ... I am able to spend 150 million shillings from my own pocket for the marriage of my son ... I have six cars, two big houses, twelve wives and sixty-seven children.' Turning to his opponents, he reminded them that they 'are not small men; they are men of big bellies like Oloitiptip (*The Weekly Review*, 30 March 1984, pp. 1–2). Forty years later the populist deputy J. M. Kariuki had absolutely no need to disguise his wealth in order to win credibility with the citizens – the 'wananchi' (see Odinga 1992, p. 63). Thus the 'politics of the belly', to use Bayart's phrase, is very much in the imagination of Kenyans and is not just a fictive creation of Ngugi.

Ngugi's intervention lies in his insistence that the 'politics of the belly' that he erects on the stage for us ought to be the object of ridicule rather than emulation. The belly, which the rulers in particular decode as a sign of success, ought to expose the parasitic nature of the local comprador in a postcolony. Thus, far from confirming their authority, the grotesque image of rulers like Oloitiptip, should serve to undermine the power of the rulers by turning them into pitiable objects of ridicule. After all, 'the body itself is the principal locale of the idioms and fantasies used in depicting power' (Mbembe 1992, p. 7). If Kenyans in their ignorance have associated 'the big belly' with power, then Ngugi is forcing them to debunk the myth, and to realise that the authority of the local rulers is borrowed.

It is, therefore, to the nature of the local comprador bourgeoisie that Ngugi draws our attention by using the grotesque mode in his depiction of them. Indeed, grotesque characters, marked as they are by bodily deficiencies or deformation, would seem to offer Ngugi a perfect means of figuring the qualities that have tended to characterise either the local comprador or the ruling elite in the postcolonial state in Africa. The use of the grotesque mode draws the readers' attention to the body as a site upon which power is contested. If the Kenyan government had intended to subdue Ngugi's body, he turns the butt on them. In *Detained*, he talks of his objective:

> I would cheat them out of that last laugh by letting my imagination loose over the kind of society this class, in nakedly treacherous alliance with imperialist foreigners, were building in Kenya in total cynical disregard of the wishes of over fourteen million Kenyans. (1981a, p. 10)

Yet, the full significance of the grotesque image in the text only makes sense when linked to a couple of subnarratives in *Devil on the Cross*.

The first of these subnarratives is derived from Wariinga's nightmare which was mentioned earlier in this chapter. In the grotesque image of the Devil that Wariinga sees, Ngugi seems to suggest a linear and continuing relationship between the Devil (read colonialism) and the black elite (read comprador bourgeoisie) that takes over at independence. Ngugi further suggests that the desire of the comprador class which rescues the Devil, thereby introducing a new form of colonialism, is to inherit the Devil's worst qualities. The second subnarrative consists of three stories that Gatuiria relates to his fellow passengers on their way to Ilmorog in a *matatu*. Common to all the stories are the themes of avarice and conceit. The first story is about the peasant farmer who was turned into a beast of burden by an ogre (Ngugi 1987, p. 62). The second story is about the black and beautiful girl who rejected all the men in her country and took to the first young man from a foreign country. The young foreigner turned out to be a man-eating ogre who tore off her 'limbs one by one and ate them' (p. 62). The third and last story that Gatuiria relates is about an old man called Nding'uri who had a soul that was richly endowed. He was well respected, hardworking and displayed neither desire nor greed for other peoples property until, one day, 'a strange pestilence attacked the village' and destroyed all his possessions (p. 63). Nding'uri was forced to turn to the evil spirits. 'At the entrance to the cave,' we read, 'he was met by a spirit in the shape of an ogre'. We are further told that the ogre

had two mouths, one on his forehead and the other at the back of his head. The one at the back of his head was covered by his long hair, and it was only visible when the wind blew the hair aside. (p. 64)

The thrust of the narrative is that Nding'uri surrenders his soul to the ogre who demands it in exchange for riches. Nding'uri is turned 'into an eater of human flesh and a drinker of human blood' (p. 64). And in a typical Bakhtinian conception of the grotesque image of the body – the body as a site for defecation – both laughable and revolting, we read that:

From that day on, Nding'uri began to fart property, to shit property, to sneeze property, to scratch property, to laugh property, to think property, to dream property, to talk property, to sweat property, to piss property. (p. 64)

If the first story by Gatuiria relates directly to the burden of colonialism on the colonised and points to the possibility of liberation from the shackles of colonialism, the second one relates to a colonial mentality – a form of cultural imperialism that locks the colonised within the orbit of dependency and leads to a fixation with all that is foreign. The third story captures the advanced stage in which the colonised now surrenders his or her being, integrity and pride to the coloniser in order to receive the protection and be schooled in the ways of the ogre. The third story is a narrative expression of the stage that Ngugi has characterised as the neocolonial stage of imperialism (1981b, p. 119–20). This is the stage that he satirises in the Devil's feast by focusing our attention on the grotesque image of the comprador class that has given up its soul and betrayed the nation for property. There is, therefore, a parallel between Wariinga's nightmare and the story of Nding'uri. Just like the Devil's rescuers in Wariinga's nightmare, Nding'uri also gives up his soul – his freedom – in exchange for property.

Significantly, both the ogre and his worshippers, like Gitutu and Kihaahu, seem to have a similar bodily deformation; they both seem to share in the common traits of avarice and conceit. Thus, every other layer of the narrative in the text serves to draw our attention to the grotesque image of the ogre, the Devil and his followers. The narrative layers serve to reveal the nature and values of the capitalist ogre and the comprador class that it gives rise to. The likes of Gitutu are born out of the ogre's womb and they continue to perpetuate its legacy, the legacy of neocolonial dependency. A section of the African elite, Ngugi seems to be saying, never contributed in the struggle for independence, but were able to prosper through sheer cunning and cheating, and by exploiting their history of collaboration to their advantage. This class, Ngugi suggests, cannot survive without the patronage of their foreign masters. Part of their fundamental weakness is that they are disposed to parasitism, selfishness, greed and naked exploitation of workers and peasants through cunning rather than creative entrepreneurship and hard work.

For Ngugi, then, the grotesque at its best exaggerates and caricatures the negative, the inappropriate, the antihuman that the comprador class has come to symbolise in his works. To this end Ngugi is in agreement with Keorapetse Kgositsile's comment that black writers should deploy the grotesque to portray 'the undesirable, the corrupting, the destructive' (1969, p. 147). But as Bakhtin argues: 'A grotesque world in which only the inappropriate is exaggerated is only quant-itatively large, but qualitatively it is extremely poor, colourless, and far from gay' (1968, p. 308).

In concluding I want to argue that in spite of Ngugi's scathing exposure of the so-called borrowed power in a postcolony, in choosing the comprador class as the sole object of his butt, Ngugi fails to draw attention to how the masses are themselves implicated in their own exploitation. By confining the display of power to the elite, and suggesting a hegemonic power structure controlled by foreign and local compradors, he fails to rise above the binary categories used in standard interpretations of domination. Within this structure, the dominated can only collaborate with or resist the rulers. And yet, as Bayart warns us,

> the production of a political space [in a postcolony] is on the one hand the work of an ensemble of actors, dominant and dominated, and ... on the other hand it is in turn subjected to a double logic of totalitarianising and detotal-itarianising ... The 'small men' also work hard at political innovation and their contribution does not necessarily contradict that of the 'big men'. (1993, p. 249)

A linear narrative of the rulers versus the ruled, the oppressor versus the oppressed, which characterises Ngugi's discourse in a postcolony runs the risk of excluding 'heterogeneity from the domain of utterance and is thus functionally incapable of even conceiving the possibility of discursive opposition or resistance to it' (Slemon 1987, p. 11). The point being made here is that in order to have an effective understanding of power relations in a postcolony, we need to realise that it cannot simply be

> a relationship of resistance or collaboration but it can best be characterised as illicit cohabitation, a relationship

fraught by the very fact of the [rulers] and [the ruled] having to share the same living space. (Mbembe 1992, p. 4)

This kind of relationship can only result in what Achille Mbembe has called the 'mutual zombification of both the dominant and those they apparently dominate' (1992, p. 4). It is a relationship of conviviality in which both the ruled and the rulers rob each other of their vitality and, in the process, render each other impotent. But because a postcolony is also a regime of pretence, the 'subjects' have to learn to bargain in this market marked by ambivalence; they have to have the 'ability to manage not just a single identity for themselves [which binarism reduces them to], but several, which are flexible enough for them to negotiate as and when required' (p. 4). It seems to me that Ngugi's otherwise brilliant critique of the rulers in a postcolony deletes the ambivalent relationship and crucial contradictions between the ruled and the rulers. In a way, it also robs the ruled of any historical agency outside the grand regime of resistance narrative.

Ngugi's Textual Counter-discourse

What emerges in Ngugi's novels is the fact that characters are used as symbols of social classes and as representatives of social groups. In the earlier novels character depiction is used to enhance certain general values and qualities that are expected to relate to some social groups in the society, while in the later novels, they are used to show that conflict is not waged among individuals or between individuals and a community but among social classes or forces. The use of the grotesque and of generic names, for example, become ways and means of figuring, not an individual character, but whole groups. The grotesque image of the body and names become signifiers that draw our attention to the values and norms of a social group or class as fixed. I have also shown that the individual's thoughts and deeds become represent-ative of his or her class and are, therefore, a reflection of what takes place in the wider society. Characters are, therefore, an important aspect of the symbolic structure within the narrative. They are allegorical to the extent that they parallel what takes place in society.

However, Ngugi tends towards a purely schematic allegorical portrayal that undermines any notion of typicality. In his later novels, he is trapped in a binary polarity within which the reading of the postcolonial situation is always suspended on the determining structure of the First World and Third World, the oppressor and the oppressed. Allegory for Ngugi would seem to be a textual counter-discourse, an anti-imperialist figurative opposition which involves the contestation and subversion of colonialist discourse and nothing more.

And yet, a counter-discourse such as Ngugi's, which positions itself as 'other' to a dominant discourse, runs the risk of excluding 'heterogeneity from the domain of utterance and is thus functionally incapable of even conceiving the possibility of discursive opposition or resistance to it' (Slemon 1987, p. 11). The kind of discourse that locates itself in direct opposition to the dominant 'other' tends to negate plurality, diversity and specific contradictions that should characterise the anticolonial narrative. Ngugi's narrative reduces history to broad analytical paradigms and figures history through static and general symbols of cognition.

3

Character Portrayal in Ngugi's Novels

One of the major thrusts of the novel tradition has been toward the creation of characters who appear to have motive and free will, and for whom we as readers posit pasts and futures which extend implicitly beyond the boundaries of the narrative. If there is one thing that Ngugi's novels, except for *Weep Not, Child* and *A Grain of Wheat,* have in common is that they do not fully partake of this tradition. Ngugi's characters tend to have a significance more typological than psychological. Their motivation for action is more often than not determined by the nature of the plot and circumscribed by the requirements of the story. Ngugi's *The River Between, Petals of Blood, Devil on the Cross* and *Matigari* could be said to display an overdetermined narrative structure which tends to develop around a predictable causal chain of events in which plot, theme and character are invariably linked to what constitutes the dominant discourse in the text.

Central to *The River Between,* for example, is the way both oral prophecy of the tribe and the saviour myth direct the plot in the narrative and in the process limit the choices available to the hero of the novel, Waiyaki. The novel in its plot structure and storyline is deeply indebted to the saviour myth. This idea of the saviour follows closely, in the main, the story of Christ: a chosen man, doing the father's will, ignored by most of his fellow men and sacrificed for the sake of others. Like the biblical Messiah, Waiyaki also acquires a special place because he comes from the lineage of great seers. If Christ came from the house of David, Waiyaki is the son of Chege,the man with the gift of magic and prophecy. People believe that Chege is the voice of Mugo. Chege himself thinks of Waiyaki as a saviour: 'He lived in the son. If the prophecy had not been fulfilled in him, well, there was the son. What was the difference? A saviour shall come from the hills' (Ngugi 1965, p. 38). Waiyaki himself begins to see himself as a saviour and a man with a mission. He has to be prepared for his mission at Siriana. Indeed, Waiyaki is convinced that the greatest mission to his people lies in the provision of education. And although he sometimes feels oppressed by his calling, he has a clear sense of messianic mission to save through education. The myth helps Ngugi in articulating his theme of public responsibility which is seen as an educated man's burden that Waiyaki must take on, a notion not very far removed from the colonial sense of mission, duty and *noblesse oblige*.

And yet Waiyaki's political vision would seem to be compromised by the overall limited vision inherent in the saviour myth as a thematic and structural framework within which Ngugi has to capture the nationalist desires of his community. The problem with a myth such as the one of the saviour is that it tells a story in such a predetermined fashion that the narrator does not have the opportunity to manipulate the plot or results. Again with such a myth, once the protagonist fails, an atmosphere of social desperation and spiritual dereliction takes over.

The narrative structure imposed by the saviour myth is such that Waiyaki has very little personal agency outside that cut out for him in nationalist rhetoric: as a modernising agent of history. And yet the modernising project that Waiyaki embraces is totally at variance with the desires of a community polarised by the advent of colonialism. He has of necessity to be constituted through a series of ambiguities and ambivalences. On the one hand he embodies a type of pure nationalism: 'Kinuthia [Waiyaki's friend] was convinced that Waiyaki was the best man to lead people, not only to a new light through education, but also to new opportunities and areas of self-expression through political independence' (Ngugi 1965, p. 118). Part of this project is to escape or free himself from 'the ritual demands of the tribe' (p. 121), part of it is to try and modernise the 'tribe' through education and provide it with a more up-to-date form of information broking than the reliance on rumour which is stressed throughout the novel as a corrosive force. But Waiyaki also has to try and inscribe his nationalism with some vestige of ethnicity and his attempts to do so are couched in the following form: 'A people's traditions could not be swept away overnight. That way lay disintegration. Such a tribe would have no roots, for a people's roots were in their traditions going back to the past, the very beginning, Gikuyu and Mumbi' (p. 141). But for us readers these sentences are problematic precisely because we know that Waiyaki's vision is premised on a modernist project which gives very little room to 'tribal' ways, even in its most radical form. Besides, the narrative logic has of necessity to propel Waiyaki towards his rejection by the community and utter alienation from their ways.

Waiyaki naively believes that modern education, even when it is imposed on a people, can lead to some form of liberation and communal unity. In the novel Kabonyi asks Waiyaki what he wants the people to do with the formal education he is so zealous to cultivate. Kabonyi then asks the rhetorical question: 'Do you think the education of the tribe, the education and wisdom which you all received, is in any way below that of the white man?' (Ngugi 1965, p. 95). Whether or not we think that Kabonyi's motivation is suspect, because of his desire to be the saviour, is beside the point. The fact of the matter is that he sees more clearly the dangers of taking on the ways of the white man uncritically. His position gestures towards Ngugi's more recent discourses on decolonisation and the restoration of community. It is what Edward Said calls 'the repossession of culture that goes on long after the political establishment of independent nation-states' (1994, p. 257).

For all its pretensions to independent status, Waiyaki's school teaches what he has learned in Siriana. Kabonyi's argument is that to follow Waiyaki is to widen the gap that already exists in the tribe by adding in general terms an alien culture to the alien religion. Neither Waiyaki nor Ngugi can give specific answers to Kabonyi's questions. The possibility of a syncretic culture can only lead them to a reversion to some questionable tribal practice in the form of female circumcision, a practice whose rejection by the missionaries and local converts subverts the very unity that Waiyaki desires. Besides how can education yield the desired unity in the face of colonial encroachment and arrogance? Waiyaki's friend and fellow teacher, Kinuthia, seems to have a better understanding of the prevailing mood in the society than him.

> Yet he wondered if Waiyaki knew that people wanted action now, that the new enthusiasm and awareness embraced more than the mere desire for learning. People wanted to move forward. They could not do so as long as their lands were taken, as long as their children were forced to work in the settled ridges, as long as women and men were forced to pay hut-tax. (Ngugi 1965, p. 118)

Clearly, the connection between education and the politics of the day that Kinuthia brings up, the burden of colonialism in the form of land alienation, forced labour and forced taxation, are all issues that are left undeveloped in the novel. It is as if Ngugi is saying that 'seek ye first the whiteman's Educational kingdom and all shall be added unto you'. Kabonyi may be malevolent, but he has his pulse at the right place: he is in touch with the demands and grievances of the community.

In resigning from the Kiama, Waiyaki also makes a political blunder because he creates room for Kabonyi's political intrigues. It is again his friend, Kinuthia who warns him of the power of the Kiama. 'Be careful, Waiyaki ... The Kiama has power. Power. And your name is in it, giving it even greater power' (Ngugi 1965, p. 112). Clearly, it is in the Kiama that one finds the seeds of the legitimate independence movement, and yet Waiyaki thinks he can bypass it. We are told that the Kiama is getting more and more power over the people, and rightly so because it touches on their real grievances. The more power the Kiama has the more isolated Waiyaki becomes. Ultimately, every action in the novel would seem to push Waiyaki towards his demise and total rejection at the hands of his people.

The question is, does Ngugi provide his hero with a spectre of choice? Could the writer manipulate the framework rooted in the saviour myth to redeem his hero and to give him greater agency? It seems to me that the inevitability of

Waiyaki's fate at the end is embedded in the structure of the narrative, and although Waiyaki in the end comes to the realisation that he should have developed the political aspect of his mission, the narrative voice is unequivocal in its condemnation of the people. In the end we are made to feel that it is the people, and not Waiyaki, that have betrayed the tribe. The people have rejected their saviour and they are ashamed: 'Neither did they want to speak to one another, for they knew full well what they had done to Waiyaki and yet they did not want to know' (Ngugi 1965, p. 152).

And yet, to be fair to Ngugi, he allows for no total narrative closure. There is no pretence that the search for the right idioms to name the nascent resistance culture has been fully realised or deleted by Waiyaki's rejection. And here Ngugi subverts the messianic myth to an extent. Far from threatening the people with the final judgement and far from hiding in the delusion of a prophecy fulfilled, Waiyaki's internal conflict continues and as Edward Said puts it: 'Ngugi powerfully conveys the unresolved tensions that will continue well after the novel ends and that the novel makes no effort to contain' (1994, pp. 254–5). This is what the narrative voice is hinting at when we are told:

> all at once Waiyaki realized what the ridges wanted. People wanted action now. Now he knew what he would preach if he ever got another chance: education for unity. Unity for political freedom. (Ngugi 1965, p. 143)

It is the weight of this political action, the unresolved tensions, that is at the heart of his subsequent novels, *Weep Not, Child* and *A Grain of Wheat*, where Ngugi gives greater spectre of choice and a much more complex character portrayal of the major protagonists. In these two novels, Ngugi is 'clearly concerned as much with "psychological consequences" as with "the theme of a people living and acting within the Mau Mau period itself"' (Nkosi 1981, p. 40). The tensions that we encounter in *The River Between*, which lead to simplistic polarisation of characters as traditionalists and Christians, assume a much more complex reading in these texts. And the principal vehicles for reading the contradictions of the specific historical conjunctures are the characters that serve to illuminate the ambiguities of the moment and the historical dilemmas engendered by the anticolonial war. Nationalism is anchored around real experiences of characters. Both past and present experiences intermingle to evoke our sympathies and to give a better understanding of the characters and of their social milieu. All characters are subjected to scrutiny and their roles assessed for what they are.

The key to Ngugi's characterisation in the two novels is the interplay he creates between repressive political structures and the individual psychology of his characters, steeped in their social background. I think it is in these two novels that Ngugi resolves what he saw as the tension between individualism and communal consciousness that plagues *The River Between*. People get inserted into historic moments in society which exact certain demands on them as part of the collective or national experience, but they also have specific histories as individuals which have a bearing on how they respond to the demands of history. If authoritarian political structures in colonial Kenya shape the perceptions of Ngugi's characters in *Weep Not, Child* and *A Grain of Wheat*, whether or not they accept the structures, the specific histories of Ngugi's characters also significantly influence their conceptions of political and social relations in a colonialist context.

Perhaps the most striking examples of Ngugi's characterisation are Ngotho and Howlands in *Weep Not, Child*. Both carry a similar baggage into the emergency. Having fought in the First World War, they are disillusioned with Britain and loathe it. Significantly, Howlands now regards Kenya as his home and, if anything, hates Britain more than Ngotho. Again they both lost promising sons in the Second World War for a country which had promised freedom and liberty for all only to revert to its repressive structures in the colony. And now both men, brought together by colonialism, have to reckon with a new war – the Mau Mau war of independence. The war thrusts new responsibilities on them, some of which Mr Howlands in particular has been running away from.

> The present that had made him a D.O. reflected a past from
> which he had tried to run away. That past had followed

him even though he had tried to avoid politics, government, and anything else that might remind him of that betrayal. (Ngugi 1964, p. 76)

Ngotho, for his part, is faced with a crisis of authority in his family and a basic loss of power. In the end when the two men die, Mr Howlands at the hands of Boro, we are profoundly moved by their tragedy. We are moved because they are presented not just as typological figures, but more importantly as human beings with personal histories with which we can identify. And here Ngugi forces us to confront the moral dilemmas engendered by a long history of imperialism, not just in Kenya, but elsewhere in the world. Imperial history is therefore judged not only by the way it destroyed the colonised subjects but also by how it afflicted psychological pain on its own people. It is the metaphor of land, the ultimate signifier of imperial history, that creates both the bond and divide between Ngotho and Mr Howlands. The two have crossed paths in the broader geographic plane of human history, but they are not just bloodless symbols of this history, they are above all human beings.

The interplay between a repressive political structure and personalised human experience acquires greater complexity in *A Grain of Wheat*. The novel is built around a shared sense of guilt and betrayal. The betrayals operate at two levels: the public betrayals in response to a repressive political structure and personal betrayals emanating from self-interest which is further compounded, in certain cases, by personal histories of fear and inadequacy. The betrayals range from the most obvious case of Karanja who once flirted with the freedom movement but later turned administrative chief for his area, to Gikonyo who broke down during his detention and broke the Mau Mau oath in order that he may come back to Mumbi, and to Mumbi herself who at the false news of Gikonyo's release gives in to Karanja's sexual advances and later bears him an illegitimate son. Indeed, even the whites get involved in one form of treachery or another. And yet, at the heart of the novel lies an even greater treachery and a larger irony which is that of Mugo: the man chosen to lead the Uhuru celebrations is actually Kihika's traitor. These betrayals gesture towards the possibility of betrayals of the ideals and goals of Uhuru by those who have assumed the reins of power in independent Kenya, and this is precisely because they are motivated by self-interest, tragic personal histories and the impact of a harsh colonial structure. Ngugi's characterisation, underpinned by the betrayal motif, is significant because it not only renders his characters profoundly human, but it also serves to undermine the false rhetorics of post-liberation politics by calling for a thorough examination of the motives and actions of our nationalist leaders.

The character through whom most of these ambiguities of the historic moment and basic human inadequacies are filtered is Mugo. Haunted by his own inadequacy, Mugo is portrayed in terms that easily elicit our sympathy. An orphan, having lost both parents at a tender age, Mugo has to remain under the custody of a cruel aunt. At a very early age, he emerges as a lonely soul, alienated from the greater community and plagued by insecurity. His loneliness drives him to escape into his piece of land, but when the emergency is declared by the British, Mugo is detained in spite of the fact that he was never really interested in the struggle. While in detention, his land is taken away and Mugo comes out devastated. As if this is not enough, the people of Thabai want to impose political leadership on him in the absence of Kihika and yet he knows that his heart is not in the struggle and he has betrayed Kihika. It is the fear that his limited space is increasingly being encroached upon that drives him to betray Kihika. And yet strictly speaking it is the repressive colonial structure that compounds Mugo's life by disrupting the lyricism that he had established between himself and his piece of land and by imposing on him certain political responsibilities that his fragile character cannot sustain. The same political system forces him to buy into its ideology of collaboration and to believe in the colonial myth that real power resides in being in a position to inflict 'pain and death to others without anyone asking questions' (Ngugi 1967, p. 197). His confession in the end marks a process of personal healing from his childhood inadequacies, but it also marks a reversal in the conception of the workings of the colonial regime. If betrayal is rooted in colonialist structures and self-interest, then the custodians of independent Kenya must reject these values. It seems to me that in his portrayal of Mugo, Ngugi was in search of a national character – not a primordial national character – but one that would be willing to lay its soul bare for the nation and to avoid the trappings of colonialist structures and personal ambition, all of which had become most apparent at the time Ngugi was writing this novel. What follows is a remarkable deviation from the complexity of character portrayal that we find in both *Weep Not, Child* and *A Grain of Wheat*. Ngugi reverts to the over-determined narrative structure in his later novels.

The Overdetermined Narrative Structure and the Victim Type in the Later Novels

This section explores Ngugi's depiction of the victim type as a character whose portrayal is predicated on and contrasted with the exploiter type we saw in the previous chapter. Ngugi relies on overdetermined narrative structure in his definition and portrayal of the victim type. Thus the types of exploiter (comprador class) and victim constitute the most important binary opposites in Ngugi's postcolonial narratives. While the exploiter embodies the values of the comprador class and capitalism, portrayed by Ngugi as serving it with religious devotion, the victim type, by contrast, embodies the values of the 'wretched of the earth' – the workers and peasants. Between these extremes we have the artist type, the vacillating intellectual. Torn between the values of his elitist background and those of the oppressed, the artist type ultimately succumbs to the bidding of the heart and betrays the struggle. The vacillating intellectuals are, in the final analysis, on the side of the oppressor. They are more individualised in their portrayal than the average Ngugi types of exploiter and victim. They are characterised by rebellion, idealism and escapism. They are also given greater latitude in terms of the choices they can make as characters. In the end, as I seek to argue, Ngugi still upholds a character typology which invites allegorical reading of characters as symbolic structures that stand for something larger than themselves.

An overdetermined narrative structure tends to develop around a predictable causal chain of events in which plot, theme and character are invariably linked to what constitutes the dominant discourse in the text. In the case of *Devil on the Cross*, class oppression by the *comprador* class within the broad dependency perspective would seem to be the dominant text, although this is also linked to gender oppression as a subtext. In the delineation of Wariinga's character as the main victim of oppression in *Devil on the Cross*, the focus is on the compounded effects of class and gender on Wariinga. And this is achieved by means of an overdetermined narrative structure, the kind that Daniel Scheiber argues, tends 'toward redundancy – the repetition or exaggeration of semic material far beyond the discourse' (Scheiber 1991, p. 265).[1] Every incident in the novel, for example, is securely linked in a causal chain that compels our attention to class and gender oppression as the source of Wariinga's predicament. Each narrative foray leads to a single point, the suffering of Wariinga. Each detail in the novel contributes its own resonance to Wariinga's tragedy, at the level of plot or symbolism.

From the beginning of the narrative, the writer focuses on Wariinga as a victim[2] whose life history demands narrative ordering. We read that the Prophet of Justice was compelled to 'reveal what now lies concealed by darkness' because 'this story was too disgraceful, too shameful, that it should be concealed in the depths of everlasting darkness' (Ngugi 1982, p. 7). The compelling voice of revelation, Julien writes, 'signals both the symbolic nature of the ensuing story, its kinship to allegory and fable, and its moral authority' (1992, p. 147). For Ngugi, Wariinga's narrative is allegorical of the state of the nation; it is a narrative about the submerged history of the oppressed which has always been suppressed in the master narrative.

Wariinga is born of parents who fight for independence, are detained and then released only to find that their land has been sold to homeguards. When Wariinga moves to a neighbouring town of Nakuru to study under the care of her aunt, she becomes victim of the Rich Old Man – her uncle's friend. By enticing the innocent and pure Wariinga with gifts, the

Rich Old Man succeeds in thwarting Wariinga's youthful ambitions to go to university because she falls pregnant. She is rejected by the man, attempts to commit suicide and is saved by Muturi, the man that later turns out to be the leader of the worker's movement. She trains as a secretary and vows never to be used again by the rich. When she joins Boss Kihara's company, she rejects the advances of Boss Kihara who hits back by firing her. For the second time, Wariinga falls victim of the rich, propertied class.

But what is perhaps significant in the narrative is the fact that Wariinga is also rejected by her boyfriend, a university student, whom she loves and on whom she spends all her money. And in this incident, Ngugi exposes the African elite as being in league with the propertied class in their exploitation of innocent women. But in a direct reflexive satire, Ngugi exposes the folly of women like Kareendi (Wariinga) who surrender themselves to men like slaves and allow men to take full advantage of them, while they remain silent and behave 'like a lamb cropping grass' (Ngugi 1982, p. 20). She attempts another suicide.

It is during the third suicide attempt in the streets of Nairobi that, in a typical narrative strategy of coincidental plots, Wariinga is brought into a forced relationship with the man who rescues her, a student leader who invites her to the Devil's feast in Ilmorog. On her way to Ilmorog she enters into a relationship with four characters, Gatuiria, Muturi, Wangari and Mwireri wa Mukiraai, that will alter her life significantly. Wariinga undergoes a metamorphosis during a spiritual trial in which she encounters a voice: a roaming spirit who opens up her whole life history and the social struggle around her. She has to make the choice between serving the Devil with all the material wealth that goes with it or fighting against the 'eaters' (Ngugi 1982, p. 188). It is after her encounter with Muturi's 'mob' of workers and students that another significant change takes place in Wariinga. She is faced with the difficult choice of having to take sides in the struggle. Muturi challenges both her and Gatuiria to use their brains in the service of the people. Indeed, it dawns upon Wariinga for the first time that as a secretary, she had sacrificed four basic things that make a whole woman: her hands, brains, humanity and thighs (Ngugi 1982, p. 206). When Muturi entrusts her with the gun – a rather ironic use of the phallic symbol as the expression of liberated womanhood, given Ngugi's self-confessed 'progressive' stand on gender politics – we are told:

> she felt courage course through her whole body. She thought that there was not a single danger in the world that she could not now look in the face. All her doubts and fears had been expelled by the secret with which Muturi had entrusted her. (p. 211)

Wariinga decides to fulfil her lifelong ambition, trains as a mechanical motor engineer and sets herself up in business. She vows never to sell her soul to the Devil for money and never again to be owned by another man. And yet, in a tragic reversal of what should have been a happy ending, with the perfect union between Gatuiria and Wariinga, Gatuiria's father turns out to be the Rich Old Man who exploited Wariinga in her youth. In this bizarre encounter between father and daughter-in-law, conceited lover and abused woman, exploiter and victim, Gatuiria is the pawn and foe, the vacillating arbiter in the complex drama of allegorical romance. Gatuiria is helpless in these circumstances.

The delineation of Wariinga according to the victim type is in keeping with the flat, projective characterisation that we associate with overdetermined narrative structures. As I have shown, Wariinga is portrayed initially as an innocent girl beset by men who are intent on exploiting her sexually. Significantly, she displays the seme of naïveté – a mark of innocence – in her relations with the Rich Old Man and the university boyfriend. But we also know that she has the semes which point to ideal love and social ambition. She gets involved with the university boyfriend and later with Gatuiria because of that deep desire for the ideal love and not for casual romantic exploits. Similarly, she trains as a mechanic to realise her childhood ambition. Within the narrative, the two semes are suppressed in favour of the naïve, innocent and helpless victim, because if they are not suppressed they would hasten her subversion or outright rejection of the trappings of unscrupulous men. Indeed, when Wariinga appears to be in control of her life as a motor-mechanical engineer, she falls victim again to the educated Gatuiria who opens up the possibility of her realising ideal love. When Wariinga readily accepts her engagement to Gatuiria, even before knowing the parents, the irony is stark – Wariinga's adaptation to her role as sexual victim still rings of innocence and naïveté. She cannot marry Gatuiria and she cannot go back to her work because the plot on which she worked with other workers has been sold to none other than Boss Kihara and his foreign friends. Thus the plot only progresses to emphasise the spectre of the victim type. And as the narrative voice confirms, Wariinga 'knew with all her heart that the hardest struggles of her life's journey lay ahead' (Ngugi 1982, p. 254).

The nature of Wariinga's story shows clearly how Ngugi works to remove the spectre of 'choice' – traditionally regarded as the prime source of character motivation – from Wariinga's actions. (In Chapter 4, I will show how Ngugi resorts to dreams, the fantastic and the journey motif to realise Wariinga's character transformation.) The heroine's fate is tied to the demands of the discourse as Ngugi asserts the inevitability of the plot's movement in a predictable direction. The plot points to the unresolved tragic conflict between the victim type and the exploiter type; it is a tragic conflict which the intellectual elite, the artist type, Ngugi would have us believe, is incapable of resolving or providing decisive intervention. Seemingly, independent agents like Gatuiria and his unknowing implication in Wariinga's tragedy help to amplify Wariinga's victimisation. The novel's highly directive structure relentlessly pushes us in two directions: toward Wariinga as a victim and, as we have already seen, toward the elite propertied class, as the source of Wariinga's tragedy. The immediate agent of Wariinga's suffering, Gitahi, is partially obscured, becoming just a foil in the structural confrontation between the capitalists and workers that Wariinga represents. That is the symbolic sig-nificance of the confrontation between Gitahi and Wariinga in which Wariinga dismisses the fatally wounded Gitahi in images we have come to associate with the grotesque in the narrative: 'There kneels a jigger, a louse, a weevil, a flea, a bedbug! He is mistletoe, a parasite that lives on the trees of other people's lives!' (Ngugi 1982, p. 254).

But Wariinga's act of revolt points to a release of a new semic energy, the trait of resistance which now underpins Wariinga's desire to realise her social ambition, constantly stifled by forces of capital and male oppression. Although the revolt is contrived, it points to Ngugi's hope in the victim type and the possibility of regeneration. We can conclude that the traits which define Wariinga's character are in complicity with the nature and the progress of the discourse. We can only understand Wariinga's character in relation to her oppression, both in terms of class and gender. Her character is contrasted to that of Gitahi or Gitutu. Gitahi, like Gitutu, is denied any positive human values, while Wariinga is endowed with positive values, but stereotypically constructed as victim to elicit our sympathy. But because Gitahi and Wariinga represent two binary polarities – evil and good, exploiter and exploited, hunter and hunted – they are both denied full humanity. They are mere symbolic structures and have a significance that is more typological than psychological: they are composed of traits which provide a necessary 'complicity' with the requirements of the discourse, and nothing more.

The Individualised Character: The Intellectual/Artist Type

Vacillating between the collaborating type – the comprador bourgeoisie – and non-collaborators – the victim type – are the intellectuals who have failed to take sides with any one of the two groups in Kenyan society. They constitute the educated elite. As Muturi, the worker leader, asserts: 'Those educated people are often not sure whose side they are on. They sway from this side to that like water on a leaf' (Ngugi 1982, p. 211). Ngugi's uncommitted intellectuals always project the image of the artist figure who adopts the status of internal exile. 'These characters', Gikandi writes of artist figures, 'exist in a world which always seems beyond their practical abilities, so that understanding is no longer the instrument of dealing with real-life experiences; they prefer to withdraw from a world which they know only too well' (Gikandi 1987, p. 74). The values to which they aspire are often in direct contradiction with the values and demands of their family or social background. For these reasons, Ngugi's artist type is always marked by rebellion, idealism and flight. But unlike the other two types already discussed, the artist is afforded some latitude of choice, a fundamental instrument for character motivation that Ngugi denies his average type. Two characters in Ngugi's corpus of narrative stand out as good examples of the artist type: Gatuiria in *Devil on the Cross* and Munira in *Petals of Blood*.

Munira and Gatuiria, just like the teacher in *Matigari* who prefers the culture of silence to active political engagement, express Ngugi's attitude and sense of disillusionment with the intellectual elite in Kenya. Ngugi portrays Munira and Gatuiria as rebels against the crass material obsession of their parents. They are unable to do anything positive to change things except for idealistic, spiritual and academic postures which lead to no practical commitment to change the status quo. Their characters are defined by the images of entrapment and escape. Munira in *Petals of Blood* is similar to Gatuiria in the way their portraits are drawn. Munira, although one of the major protagonists and one of the narrators in *Petals of Blood*, remains a detached intellectual like Gatuiria. He is a confused rebel hating his father's lifestyle on the one hand and secretly wishing to be a lord, a master and owner on the other hand. He is filled with feelings of failure and inadequacy. He is detached, isolated and wants to remain uninvolved and neutral. Munira is entrapped within the classroom walls. He finds refuge in teaching and ultimately takes to religion as a means to escape from reality. Gatuiria is trapped in endless research and an escapist indulgence in the so-called African music which he fails to relate to reality.

These characters also have associations with the heroes and heroines of their stories which are tinged with tragedy. Munira's father turned Karega's mother into a slave and drove Munira's sister, a girlfriend of Karega, to suicide. Gatuiria's father was Wariinga's 'sugar-daddy' who destroyed her in her innocent youth. Gatuiria's portrait will suffice to illustrate the nature and behaviour of this character type.

Gatuiria, whose name simply means 'the seeker' or 'the quester', is portrayed by Ngugi as having some revolutionary potential and to that extent much of the novel's hope is pinned on him. He is poised to take sides with the oppressed majority when he rejects his father's property in youthful rebellion. Sent abroad by the father to study a 'relevant' degree in Business Studies, Gatuiria rebels again and studies African music. On his return, he commits himself to the restoration of African culture through research in African music. Like Achebe the novelist, he sets out to find where 'the rain began to beat us' (Achebe 1973, p. 3) and to redress the cultural inequities of colonial Kenya. The product of his two years of research work in music is an oratorio which tells the story of the nation. We are told that Gatuiria could

> even visualize the audience surging out of the concert hall, angry at those who sold the soul of the nation to foreigners and babbling with joy at the deeds of those who rescued the soul of the nation from foreign slavery. Gatuiria hopes that above all, his music will inspire people with patriotic love for Kenya. (Ngugi 1982, p. 227)

Apparently, Gatuiria intends the musical composition to be his engagement gift to Wariinga. In an allegorical sense, this act of love and passion would symbolise patriotism and commitment to the nation. Thus Gatuiria's romantic commitment to Wariinga, the despised and abused woman, is to be read as a patriotic commitment to the nation with music which is part of Kenya's heritage as the symbolic expression of this commitment. Gatuiria's involvement with African music is his way of dealing with his alienation and a way of reconciling himself to the roots of his peoples' culture. Music thus becomes an instrument for healing angst and a form within which meaning can be realised in the fragmented world that surrounds him. It is also his way of rejecting the values of his background and the demands of his father, which are steeped in the power of materialism and ignore the spiritual processes that have shaped the destiny of his people over the years.

What Gatuiria forgets is that he is himself caught between the mortar and the pestle: the values steeped in African heritage that he aspires to and the values acquired through his elitist education which are steeped in Western values. And indeed, right from the beginning, the narrator is at pains to demonstrate that Gatuiria is in fact a hybrid of sorts, always mixing English and Gikuyu words (Ngugi 1982, p. 38). His ideas on Africa's cultural life are but fragmented memories of material cultures buried in the past of his people. Gatuiria calls for a retrieval of cultural values he can relate to only remotely; they are like the riddles he used to listen to in the past and can no longer solve, even the simplest of them (pp. 57–8). His search is therefore marked by a sense of idealism that is not grounded in practical experience. And herein lies Gatuiria's ineffectiveness: he has composed many songs, he tells his fellow passengers in the *matatu*, but he has 'not yet found the tune or the theme of the music of [his] dreams' (p. 59). Gatuiria's self-conscious acknowledgement of his dilemma is best captured in his inability to come to Wariinga's rescue or to do anything concrete.

> Gatuiria did not know what to do, to deal with his father's body, to comfort his mother or to follow Wariinga. So he just stood in the middle of the courtyard, hearing in his mind music that led him to nowhere. (p. 254)

Thus, Ngugi would have us believe, Gatuiria the intellectual fails in love, fails in patriotism and fails in commitment at the hour of need. He fails to take his logical place; he fails to take sides with Wariinga the abused and deprived woman and Ngugi's true expression of nationhood. Gatuiria fails to perform the music of his dreams. He fails to render the great oratorio meant to be a celebration of his people's culture, but more importantly, he misses the opportunity to make a statement against people like his father who had 'sold the soul of the nation to foreigners' (p. 227).

But Gatuiria's predicament is not as unproblematic as the narrative seems to imply. It is also not correct to argue, like Gichingiri Ndigirigi, that 'Gatuiria fails because he undertakes to write a revolutionary song as an academic pursuit without immersing himself in the lives of those he writes about and taking sides with them' (1991, p. 105). Ndigirigi seems to imply that Gatuiria's composition is written for the oppressed and not with them (as producers and consumers), a problematic which would seem to point to Ngugi's recent shifts with regard to theatre, in which he argues for theatre and cultural activity as a communal experience; a collective process in which the workers and peasants are to be involved in the production and consumption of artistic experience (Ngugi 1986, p. 41).

Ndigirigi's position, which echoes Ngugi's recent rhetorics on new directions in African theatre, rests on the complacent assumption that the category of the intellectual elite is an uninscribed and unproblematic space, whose only moment of social agency is locked up with the struggles of the masses. But it is important to deal with the African intellectual as a unique and specific category that need not be understood in relation to the struggles of the masses or judged purely in terms of how best they articulate the broad issues of the oppressed. In my view, Gatuiria's indecisiveness and his so-called lack of commitment to the struggle is more than an act of reaction, but a tragic expression of a vacillating and ambiguous attitude of intellectuals in Africa towards a system in which they are both pawns and beneficiaries. This is the savage irony of the position of the African intellectual in the postcolonial state. Thus Gatuiria's search cannot simply be reduced to an ordinary academic quest as Ndigirigi and Ngugi attempt to do. It is a genuine situation of conflict which cannot be resolved by taking sides in some undefined struggle, even when this is done in the name of the masses.

Besides, at a personal level, Gatuiria's inability to act is in many ways similar to that of Shakespeare's Hamlet. In both cases the protagonists are faced with extremely difficult choices and the circumstances calling for partisan action remain ambiguous and fraught with tragic consequences. The ambiguities referred to here are both human and political.

Gatuiria is faced with the difficult choice of having to take sides either with his girlfriend, or to abandon his mother at this critical moment. Either way the choice is not easy. Indeed, even the political struggle Gatuiria is called upon to join hangs on a very thin thread, with only Muturi and Wariinga as symbols of its tenuous presence.

There is no doubt that the portrait of the spineless intellectual who is the artist type is the most well drawn of all Ngugi's characters. He demonstrates a deep psychological insight into their lives and brings out their social circumstance in a realistic manner. Their thoughts and actions, and the forces which have conditioned them, are vividly painted. And more than any other type, they have greater latitude in making a choice that is not entirely subordinated to the demands of the discourse. Gatuiria, like the seeker that he is, interrogates the social processes and raises questions to a greater extent than any other character in the *matatu* taxi and in the entire narrative. Indeed, the stories of ogres that he relates to his fellow passengers turn out to be at the heart of the text's central concern. Gatuiria is the embodiment of the contradictions of a world of which he is barely in control, a world to which he cannot give meaning or a harmonious tune.

Indeed, as Ian Glenn argues, the intellectual characters for Ngugi play a mediating role in the postcolonial state and their predicament 'is structurally related to that of the élite whose alienation is paradoxically their source of power' (Glenn 1981, p. 63). Glenn argues that there is a homological relationship between the intellectual protagonists in Ngugi's novels and the intellectual elite in postcolonial Kenya. Thus, one would conclude that Gatuiria and Munira are allegorical figures, but more complex ones than the two types we have discussed previously, which Ngugi uses to mediate the role of the uncommitted intellectual in Kenya. In a way, Ngugi understands them best because they are homologous to his own position as an intellectual. But this, notwithstanding, Ngugi's characters remain fixed archetypes of social types: the exploiter and the victim; the collaborator and the resister; the robber and the robbed. Thus, Ngugi's 'homeguard', his spineless intellectual and his revolutionary heroine and victim remain more or less the same in most of his novels.

4

The Use of Popular Forms and the Search for Relevance

One of the most important developments in Ngugi's narrative in recent years has been his creative use of orality in his post-colonial discourses in Kenya. Indeed, ever since his publication of *Petals of Blood*, Ngugi has been troubled by the fact that he could not readily communicate with his target audience, the workers and peasants whose lives fed his novels. 'I knew whom I was writing about', he asserted, 'but whom was I writing for?' (1986, p. 72). Ngugi's dilemma has been that the realist tradition within which most of his earlier novels are steeped is both complex and alienating for the purposes of his narrative, whose primary objective is to present the marginalised groups in Kenya with an alternative history.[1] Through his experimentation with the Kamiriithu popular theatre Ngugi came to believe that the answer to his dilemma lay in the popular forms steeped in the traditions and contemporary experiences of the Gikuyu: 'In search of the image that would capture the reality of a neo-colony that was Kenya under both Kenyatta and Moi, I once again fell on the oral tradition' (1986, p. 80).

Ngugi therefore decided to write in his mother tongue[2] and to use what he believes are oral narrative strategies and authentic oral forms of the Gikuyu.[3] However, the question arises as to what exactly the nature of this oral tradition is. Is Ngugi's use of the oral traditions of his people entirely new? A closer look at Ngugi's earlier novels will show that Ngugi has always been indebted to Agikuyu oral tradition and his latest shift in the works written in Gikuyu should be seen, at least in the sense of appropriating oral forms, not so much as a rupture but a continuation and a more radical development towards a syncretic use of both Gikuyu and Western modes of creation.

This chapter will therefore attempt to show that although Ngugi's recourse to oral forms is more pronounced in his works written in Gikuyu, his earlier works have always been rooted in both popular mythology – the popular forms of the Gikuyu – and a fusion of modern Western conventions of writing. Thus, the fusion between oral and written forms is not something entirely new in Ngugi's writing. The fundamental difference in the two phases in Ngugi's writing is that it anticipates different types of audiences at each phase. In the earlier novels, Ngugi is addressing himself to the English-speaking readers, both at home and abroad, while in his latest novels he is targeting the Gikuyu readers. In regard to his novels in Gikuyu, I make the point that although Ngugi presents his use of oral forms as authentic, these forms are clearly synthetic. In addition to the manifold written influences on his work, Ngugi has hinted at the fact that he was also influenced by oral traditions from other communities in Kenya and by the written traditions of the West. In *Decolonising the Mind* (1986, pp. 80–1), he mentions the influence of the human-shaped rocks of Idakho, a sub-ethnic group among the Abaluhia of western Kenya, whose images fused with the 'Marimu characters' which are 'the man-eating ogres in Gikuyu orature'. The Faust theme – the story of a man who surrenders his soul to evil as in Marlowe's *Faustus*, Goethe's *Faust*, Thomas Mann's *Dr Faustus* and Bulgakov's *Master and Margarita* – all seem to have had relevance for Ngugi's novel enterprise (pp. 80–1). The mythical redeemer who, like Matigari, could change his shape into anything also has its equivalents among the Luos and the Abaluhia ethnic groups in Kenya. But first I take a brief look at the use of oral tradition in Ngugi's earlier novels.

The Use of Oral Tradition in Ngugi's Earlier Novels

The Agikuyu myth of origin is one of the most recurring icons in Ngugi's narrative. It seems to be the cornerstone of Ngugi's art and it occurs in virtually all his novels, although it is most prominent in his earlier novels. In the second chapter I have argued that Ngugi marshalls the Agikuyu oral mythology in his nationalist imaginings. Indeed, the precolonial history is constructed entirely through a religious myth of origin. The Agikuyu myth of origin in *Weep Not, Child, The River Between* and *A Grain of Wheat* is imbued with religious connotations that represent cosmic forces that play a central role in the creation and evolution of humanity from nothing to something. Gikuyu and Mumbi also humanise a world that would otherwise be the domain of abstract and inanimate objects. The legendary Gikuyu couple has a close association with Mount Kenya, possibly the small hill to which Chege takes his son Waiyaki to reveal to him the secrets of the tribe. This hill, Mount Kenya, is the resting place of their creator and deity, Murungu – elsewhere called Ngai, *Mwenenyaga*. Mount Kenya becomes the centre of the Gikuyu universe, now under the threat of colonialism. The oral transmission of the myth from generation to generation underscores its historical significance to the community. If the belief enhances communal and spiritual unity, the mountain concretises it with a physical presence that defies time. The mountain therefore symbolises the encapsulation of the material and spiritual, the concrete and abstract, in the people. In other words, it represents their life and its continuity: after all, God, the creative essence, reposed there. Thus, if the divine powers of God are permanent, then the permanence of the mountain confirms its eternity. The myth of origin therefore has history, legend, narrative and social life all interlocked. For Ngugi, the weaving of all these genres around Mount Kenya was part of an everlasting search for an enduring moral centre.

In *The River Between* we are told that when he created Gikuyu and Mumbi, the original parents of the tribe, Murungu, the great God, told them: 'This land I give to you, O man and woman. It is yours to rule and till, you and your posterity' (Ngugi 1965, p. 2).

If Ngugi's earlier texts can be said to be a fictional examination of the consequences of the alienation of the people from their land, then in a significant way they are also an investigation into the people's alienation from their spiritual lives. This is because Murungu's promise is compromised by the coming of the whites, which has been prophesied by Mugo wa Kibiro, a great Gikuyu sage: 'There shall come a people with clothes like butterflies', he warned (Ngugi 1965, p. 2). Mugo wa Kibiro was ignored by his people in his own day just as his later-day heir, Chege, has been. It is not until the Christian Siriana missionary centre is established that Chege's people accept the reality of the prophecy. The colonial penetration of Gikuyu land in *A Grain of Wheat* is also seen as a fulfilment of a local prophecy by Mugo wa Kibiro who spoke of the coming of the iron snake. In a significant way, it is Ngugi's recourse to oral mythology that helps to naturalise his nationalist discourses in the earlier narrative. The myth of origin, while Gikuyu-specific, is a staple of any nationalist framework and hence must be seen to carry a double meaning. It is, for example, used here to naturalise the birth of the Agikuyu nation, and by extension the Kenyan nation. The phenomenon of a nation, instead of being manufactured, a socially constructed idea, becomes a natural process. Myth here becomes a legitimising ideology which transcends historicity. Significantly, all the texts of Ngugi, in spite of their obvious differences, tend to forge a spiritual link between the people and the land. In *Weep Not, Child*, Ngotho reminds his children that 'God showed Gikuyu and Mumbi all the land and told them: "This land I hand over to you. O Man and woman / It's yours to rule and till in serenity sacrificing / Only to me, your God, under my sacred tree ..."' (Ngugi 1964, p. 24).

This natural process of land acquisition, through a filial bond with the spiritual guardians of land as the ancestral spirits, is one form of creating a collective identity – a crucial staple for nationalist discourse. Thus, in Ngugi's earlier texts the collective identity, as a template for nationalist politics, is forged through the language and idiom of oral tradition, specifically through the creation myth and ancient prophecy of men like Mugo wa Kibiro. The texts allude to Mount Kenya as the privileged carrier of nationalist meaning.

And yet it is not exactly correct to argue that Ngugi's nationalist moorings are entirely constituted around the Agikuyu myth of origin. As early as his first novel, Ngugi was already stretching the meaning of orality to embrace popular forms, such as biblical allusions that had become part of the contemporary culture of the Gikuyu and of Kenya in general.

And in appropriating both Agikuyu and Christian mythology, Ngugi was striving for a hybrid form that remains the chief characteristic of his works, including the later novels in Gikuyu. His earlier novels in particular reflect the integral use of biblical allusions and Christian mythology in the novel.

Significantly, Ngugi's first novel in terms of its conception and writing was originally entitled *The Black Messiah*. The novel which was later named *The River Between* is significant in the sense that it introduces the messianic vision which dominates all his novels to date. It is also a novel that draws attention to the relevance of cultural synthesis. It explores the possibilities of creating a syncretic culture through a fusion of Christian mythology (read Western culture) and Agikuyu mythology (read African culture). Waiyaki stands precisely between these two worlds as the symbol of this syncretic possibility, offering a third discourse in the form of African nationalism. The muted theme of sacrifice in *The River Between* is developed better in *A Grain of Wheat*. This notion of sacrifice is embodied in the character of Kihika who pays the ultimate price when he is hanged by the colonialists. Again Ngugi is quick to appropriate the Bible and in the very first caption we read: 'Thou fool, that which thou sowest is not quickened, except it die.' And the first two chapters dramatise this sacrifice. The emphasis is on sowing of seeds which would die in order to bear grain. Ngugi's earlier narratives are steeped in both traditional and Christian mythology, with the tone often ranging from that of a biblical prophet to a traditional oral Gicaandi player that we encounter in *Devil on the Cross*.

Ngugi's text is therefore about the forging of a new Kenyan culture by moving away from organicist or essentialist notions of culture. The new culture will of necessity involve a process of appropriation and transformation of Western mythology to serve the needs of a contemporary Kenyan community. This is what Kihika does when he reinterprets Christianity in order to encourage Kenyans to unite and to fight, and if necessary die. He transforms the individualist conception of Christ into a collective: 'Everybody who takes the Oath of unity to change things in Kenya is a Christ. Christ then is not one person. All those who take up the cross of liberating Kenya are the true Christs for us Kenyan people' (Ngugi 1967, p. 95). As Caminero-Santangelo observes: 'While drawing on and reconfiguring the symbolism of Christ as a figure who suffers and struggles for others, Kihika magnifies the collectivity suggested in that symbolism. In doing so, he is able to take a European religion and transform it into an inspiration for the struggle for a free Kenya' (1998, p. 148).

In *A Grain of Wheat* Ngugi seems to be suggesting that Kenya is evolving a revolutionary culture whose development is contingent upon the fusion between oral tradition of the people and those from Europe as long as the local is not subordinated to Western cultural form. What Ngugi does is to strategically appropriate those Western forms that have come with colonialism and have become part of the people's popular culture. And even though the reception of the novel is confined to a limited audience due to the English language Ngugi uses, it is still the best medium for narrating the story of the nation at this particular historical conjuncture because a strictly oral story would not work.

Redefining Oral Tradition in the Agikuyu Novel

Writing about the reception of *Devil on the Cross* among the Agikuyu peasant readers, Ngugi described the process as 'the appropriation of the novel into the oral tradition' because the book was read in groups and it generated comments and discussions (Ngugi 1986, p. 83).[4] Ngugi was, in fact, appropriating oral and popular forms into the novel and thus striving towards a hybrid form because he still had to reconcile oral discourse with the written form. In the process, he is redefining orality and subordinating it to the demands of the written form. But he is also stretching the meaning of orality to embrace popular forms, such as biblical allusions that have become part of the contemporary culture of the Agikuyu and of Kenya in general. He is attempting to harness other forms of popular discourse, such as rumour – a widely accepted vehicle for expression in both oral and politically oppressed communities where free speech is suppressed. For Ngugi, then, orality is not just, in Eileen Julien's words, 'a bulwark to inspire confidence or action by association with a people's past grandeur or wisdom and virtue' (1992, p. 146), but a contemporary vehicle for meaning. Orality for Ngugi is a popular form; a medium that is accessible to his audience (Ngugi 1986, p. 77). It is a medium 'intelligible to the broad masses, adopting and enriching their forms of expression, assuming their standpoint' (Jameson 1977, p. 82). This is what Ngugi means when he talks of 'oral tradition'. He uses oral tradition to characterise a form that 'is best understood as a functional discourse which can legitimate or subvert the existing power structures of society' (Desai 1990, p. 66). Thus, for Ngugi, oral tradition is not something quiescent, but an expression of a dynamic culture embedded in the past and present experiences of a community. It is inextricably bound to popular culture – which as Tony Bennet argues is 'a site – always changing and variable in its constitution and organization' (1986, p. 98). Thus, the pull towards oral tradition for Ngugi was not just a narrow reversion to nationalist aesthetics, as Brenda Cooper argues (1992, p. 173), but a major political intervention. Ngugi was in search of a form that would help him re-establish a link with his audience – the majority of the Kenyan people for whom he was writing. For Ngugi this link had been severed in part by colonial education, which attempted to replace local forms of aesthetic expression with a new tradition. Ngugi himself as a Western-educated intellectual was heir to this colonial literary tradition.[5]

By returning to popular forms, Ngugi hopes to transcend his own literary reification and, more importantly, to use his art as a tool for political pedagogy. He is attempting to appropriate those elements of popular forms that lend themselves to didactic writing: elements that would enable Ngugi the writer and activist to capture the postcolonial experience in Kenya, which in Ngugi's own words is stranger than fiction.[6] Various possibilities are afforded to the writer by his transposition of oral forms into written narrative: to use a personal story, such as Wariinga's in *Devil on the Cross*, which is steeped in the popular culture of the Agikuyu; and to have a fuller exploration of the postcolonial state in Kenya within a larger narrative framework. It also affords him the opportunity for rich intertextuality between the written narrative and popular forms which the community still uses to explain itself.

Ngugi's use of orality draws our attention to the present, and his recent texts, which are a product of his new theoretical stance, would seem to deconstruct the notion of orality as authentically African. It is in this sense of reconceptualising orality that I find Eileen Julien's recent study, *African Novels and the Question of Orality* (1992), useful in understanding Ngugi's texts originally written in Gikuyu. Julien argues that the use of oral narrative genres is not a necessary or inherent feature of the African novel, but rather a flexible tool in the hands of the modern African writer which can be deployed to solve aesthetic and ideological problems imaginatively. The value of Julien's study lies in her nuanced articulation of orality as a complex expression of how narrative genres can be transformed in the service of the author's goals and his or her immediate sociopolitical agenda. Commenting on Ngugi's *Devil on the Cross*, Julien writes that oral language for Ngugi 'is a quality of Kenyan culture now' and not a tool for decoding the past (1992, p. 143). She adds:

> Oral language is thus not the object of representation that can be read as quaint and *passeiste* [of the past]. Orality here means the language and tradition in which this narrative is articulated, the medium in which Ngugi's audience will hear this story. (1992, p. 145)

Although the narrative strategies which Ngugi uses are not entirely peculiar to oral narrative, they are a hybrid form that creates the illusion of orality. It is these putative oral narrative strategies which open up both aesthetic and ideological possibilities for Ngugi and enable him to make a break with the conventions of realism that have shaped his earlier narrative without oversimplifying his subject and undermining the quality of his message. Of particular interest in this chapter is the way Ngugi uses apparent oral narrative techniques in motivating and engendering social transformation in his characters; and the way in which he uses oral narrative strategies to enhance the credibility of his characters as agents of change and to give force to the ideological message embedded in his narrative. In this novel enterprise, Ngugi deploys a number of putative oral narrative strategies and the most outstanding of these elements include, among others, the use of traditional seers or prophets or singer-musicians; the use of the journey or quest motif, rumour and gossip and fantastic and biblical allusions.

Following from Julien's theoretical premise, I will argue in this chapter that Ngugi uses the above hybrid elements with deliberate aesthetic intent in the articulation of his characters as the allegorical symbols of the dominant discourse in *Devil on the Cross* and *Matigari*. I seek here to demonstrate that although Ngugi's characters are largely one-dimensional beings, his invention of popular narrative strategies enables him to reconcile the tension between the grotesque characters and the realistic world which these characters inhabit; the strategies enable him to portray the kind of characters which mediate the absurdity of the postcolonial experience in Kenya, while underscoring the moral imperative of his texts. Ngugi's characters in *Devil on the Cross* and *Matigari* straddle the thin line between the real and the surreal.

The Interface Between Orality and the Written

Although in *Petals of Blood* Ngugi uses multiple points of view in the narrative, in *Devil on the Cross* and *Matigari* he opts for a common ground between oral and written narratives. He employs the point of view that is commonly used in both oral and written narratives, that is, third person narrative. Ngugi adopts the narrative style of a master griot or the traditional Agikuyu singer by using the authoritative voice of a collective narrator in an effort to create an epic atmosphere around his narratives. In *Devil on the Cross*, he assumes the role of a village prophet, a Gicaandi player in the traditional Agikuyu community. But the title 'Prophet of Justice' that is also assigned to the narrator is reminiscent of the biblical prophets whose teachings have been appropriated into the local religious traditions of the Agikuyu. In *Matigari*, the writer becomes the people's story-teller, recreating and reinterpreting a story that is steeped in the community's experience and tradition. But this story, which is otherwise part of the popular tradition, is used to mediate the contemporary Kenyan experience. Thus, in both *Devil on the Cross* and *Matigari*, we have intimate narrators; they are close to the situation precisely because they are part of the community whose experience they are narrating. The stories in the two texts are narrated by the extra-diegetic voice, who in turn employs the device of a story-teller and in the process invokes audience participation in the written narrative. What emerges is a clear recognition on the part of Ngugi that the story-teller shapes historical experience and that the narrator can intervene in real life. Thus, when he tells the story of Wariinga and Matigari, Ngugi is not just reproducing two oral narratives as received intact, but he gives an analysis of the woes of the postcolonial state in Kenya and the social problems to which the postcolonial power relations give rise. In other words, the experience of the Kenyan peasants and workers in the postcolonial state are reconstituted within a narrative framework which contextualises the experience for the reader and transcribes what was otherwise common knowledge, embedded in tradition and contemporary experience, into the written form.

In both *Devil on the Cross* and *Matigari*, Ngugi opts for the intrusive narrator because it enables him not only to report but also to comment on the narrative events and characters that inhabit his fictional world. Ngugi is so conscious of the acts of telling and listening that he draws our attention to how the two texts should be read. In *Matigari* he asserts the story's fluidity in time and space and compels the listeners to accept his mode of reception before he can tell his story. The story, Ngugi tells us, is 'based partly on an oral story about a man looking for a cure for an illness' and in his quest for the healer Ndiiro, he 'undertakes a journey of search' (1987, p. vii). Ngugi deliberately sets the tone for the quest motif which underpins the story of Matigari while at the same time pointing to the centrality of the oral medium in his latest narrative. In *Devil on the Cross* the narrator asserts the authority of his message by calling himself the Prophet of Justice, a Gicaandi player and therefore the voice of the people which is the voice of God. Julien writes that 'the narrator's voice is mobilized both in response to the call of other human voices and in response to a deeper spiritual impulse' (1992, p. 147). As a prophet, the burden of prophecy forces him to narrate the story of Wariinga and to 'reveal all that is hidden' (Ngugi 1982, p. 7). In *Matigari* the writer becomes the people's story-teller, retelling and reinterpreting the age-old story that has been passed from one generation to another. The story has a primary text, but Ngugi also creates and wills new meanings out of it and calls upon his audience to stretch the story out and to break the boundaries of its creation: 'Reader/listener: may the story take place in the country of your choice!' (Ngugi 1987, p. ix). Thus Ngugi intimates that the story-telling is a weaving process that involves both the narrator and the target audience. As with most oral narratives that seek to put forward a moral standpoint, the accent is on the story as a complex process with layers of meaning rather than the narrative as the articulation of characters and their complexity. The only difference here is that the oral performance affords the participants understanding because of visual presentation which is eliminated in the written narrative. And yet Ngugi stylises after the oral narrative in an attempt to create the illusion of orature in the novels – an illusion that would be impossible within the framework of a conventional novel. Thus, in Ngugi, the written narrative is presented as if it were an oral narrative with an imaginary listening audience. In other words, in Ngugi's *Devil on the Cross* and *Matigari* '[t]he story intimates a telling between the speaker–writer and the listener–reader, and inside that telling–listening there are, as Bakhtin would have it, other tellers and listeners' (Julien 1992, p. 145). Thus, in deploying this oral mode, Ngugi would seem to be more interested in the story and his audience's emotional involvement with the story rather than with character delineation. Within this problematic, Ngugi seems to have abandoned the collective narrator, the 'we' voice that mediated the experience in *Petals of Blood*. Ngugi's apparent assumption is that the traditional singer–story-teller, as the omniscient narrator, stands for the collective; he or she narrates and dramatises the communal experience. After all, as in the case of *Devil on the Cross*, the narrator's authority has been established; as reader–listeners we cannot question his moral authority nor his social credibility, which is shown to be beyond reproach at the beginning of the narrative.

Ngugi also uses the third person narrative to explore the lives of the major protagonists whose experiences are representative of a community's history. In doing this, he resorts again to the traditional oral narrative technique of the journey to foreground the trials of the characters and to explore the process of social transformation in their lives. The journey motif has been used in a whole range of texts which are allegorical in nature and are aimed at serving a didactic purpose, such as Bunyan's *The Pilgrim's Progress*. In such texts the journey provides the structure within which characters, particularly the main protagonist, come to social awareness and accept the burden of their moral responsibility; it is a moment of recognition and knowledge that comes with growth. Although the journey motif has been incorporated into many written narratives, it has always been associated with oral tales in its generic use. According to Ngugi (1986, p. 77), the concept of a journey would be familiar to many ordinary Kenyans and lends itself to a simple structure. The journey motif is, therefore, transformed into a contemporary medium in Ngugi's postcolonial narratives.

The traditional use of the journey motif is normally marked by three major phases: the initiatory phase; the transformation phase; and the phase of return. Ngugi's use of this literary element can be traced back to *Petals of Blood*. Karega's initiation takes place at Siriana, where he leads a strike as a neophyte, and he continues with this phase as a teacher in Ilmorog. Karega's transformation does not take place until he undertakes the long, winding journey across Kenya. When he returns to Ilmorog, he is mature, his politics have changed. He is now able to articulate his vision for the future and to provide leadership for the workers who discover in him good leadership qualities.

Wariinga's narrative, in *Devil on the Cross*, is also conceived in terms of a journey. Wariinga, as Ngugi himself has observed, undertakes two 'main journeys over virtually the same ground' (1986, p. 77). She moves in a *matatu* taxi from the capital city Nairobi to the fictional rural outpost of Ilmorog. Wariinga also makes a second journey in a car from

Nairobi to Ilmorog and to Nakuru. But a gap of two years separates the two journeys which parallel the stages of trans- formation in the life of Wariinga. And by the time we meet Wariinga in the final phase she has gone through a number of experiences which have transformed her life drastically. As the narrator observes: 'This Wariinga is not the one we met two years ago' (Ngugi 1982, p. 216). She is not Wariinga who was secretary and victim of Boss Kihara; she is not the innocent schoolgirl cheated and ravaged by the Rich Old Man; she is not dependent on anyone; she is 'Wariinga, our engineering hero!'; she is 'Wariinga, heroine of toil' (p. 217). And as the narrator adds, her heroism was discovered 'in the battle of life' (p. 217). She has learnt to act on her own; she has grown 'into a lucid, decisive woman' (Julien 1992, p. 151).

Matigari's quest runs at two levels. The initial movement is away from home into the forest in search of freedom and his subsequent journeys to a foreign land from where he returns to claim his house and land. Having fought colonialism, he returns to discover that injustice still exists, albeit in the form that reflects the harsh realities of the postcolonial state – a pale shadow of what he fought for. At any rate, Settler Williams and his servant John Boy whom he had fought to the death in the forest have been replaced by their sons, now partners in a leading business enterprise that exploits workers. Inspired by his experience, Matigari returns with a spiritual quest for 'Truth and Justice'. During this new quest he meets a number of allegorical figures: Guthera and the orphaned boy Muriuki, the police, the absurd Minister of Truth and Justice, the worker leader Ngaruro wa Kiriro and the people. Matigari's quest leads him to the conclusion that '[t]he enemy can never be driven out by words alone, no matter how sound the argument' (Ngugi 1987, p. 138).

It seems to me that the journey motif helps Ngugi to achieve two things: it enables him to move freely within time and space and still manage to work within a simple plot structure. It also enables him to effect social transformation in the character of his protagonists without having to provide sufficient motivation for them. As Gay Clifford says, the journey, quest or pursuit in the allegorical narrative is the 'metaphor by which a process of learning for both protagonist and readers is expressed' (1974, p. 11). Thus, the journey provides a structural framework for growth and development of character and theme within Ngugi's narrative. Character here becomes important only in so far as it elucidates the theme and mediates meaning. The growth and development of character also becomes linear and less complex in keeping with the simple plot structure within which interiority is impossible.

Thus, different phases of the journey point to important moments in the life of characters, moments which in themselves serve to illuminate not just the changes taking place in the life of individual characters, but more importantly, are a pointer to the writer's theme and a celebration of the ideal moment in a community's life. The ideal is always the hero's homecoming to liberate and gather the family together. This struggle is initiated by Karega during his return to Ilmorog where he organises the workers. It is also marked by Wariinga's return to Nakuru where she lost her virginity and where she takes her revenge on Gitahi. Matigari also returns after years of struggle in the forest to reclaim his house and land. Symbolically, Matigari's actions point to the possibility of a national rebirth and to the emergence of a new nation from the ruins of colonial and subsequent neocolonial plunder. Ngugi celebrates this possibility of the new nation, still subterranean, when Matigari marries Guthera and takes the orphaned boy, Muriuki, into his care. Coming with greater awareness from his journeys, Matigari gives Guthera and the young boy something to live for. He creates in them the vision for a better society, free of exploitation and human degradation. He gives them basic awareness and plays a crucial role in the transformation of their characters.

To encapsulate, the journey motif is an important element in an allegorical narrative such as Ngugi's. Its central function is to transport the protagonist or the character from one level of awareness or state of ignorance to a higher level of understanding and clarity of social vision. Linked to the element of movement in the development of character is the use of the fantastic, rumour and biblical allusions in character motivation. I will now discuss these elements in brief.

The Fantastic, Rumour and Biblical Allusions

Daniel Kunene, in his discussion of Mofolo's use of the fantastic, defines this device as the expression of anything 'ominous'; as something which defies our sense of the ordinary and 'our accepted system of logic' (1989, p. 186). The fantastic in life is not predictable and neither are we capable of manipulating and controlling it. Kunene continues:

> In the wake of a fantastic or miraculous event, man's role is to decode, to listen and obey. For this is knowledge revealed by that greater power, as against naturally acquired knowledge, with the express intention that it shall move those who experience it to certain types of behaviour. (p. 186)

The fantastic, as Kunene argues, is used a great deal in didactic writing 'in order to add to the persuasive power of the message or to enhance the dramatic impact of the words, or both' (p. 180). But, as Kunene adds, the fantastic 'is often regarded as being more persuasive in motivating a character to action than the ordinary logic of events' (p. 187).

Ngugi deploys the extraordinary to motivate and create awareness in the characters where the ordinary logic of events within the narrative cannot provide for either character motivation or development or both. In *Devil on the Cross*, Ngugi uses voices and dreams in the character portrayal of Wariinga. Ngugi starts by establishing the postcolonial context on which the narrative structure hinges, through Wariinga's dreams and visions. First, Wariinga, in her dream, sees the murder of Mwireri wa Mukiraai which foreshadows the elimination of the national bourgeoisie by forces of international capital in collaboration with the comprador bourgeoisie. Second, and more importantly, Wariinga sees in her dream the Devil's death and resurrection, an 'extended parable of neo-colonial dependency' (Cooper 1992, p. 52).

The heroine's experiences are thus explored within the specific historic and structural frame of neocolonial dependency in Kenya; a framework that is established in the first instance through Wariinga's dreams and visions. In Wariinga's case, the voices manifest themselves on the threshold of her consciousness and lead to basic choices that she makes; choices which help in the advancement of her social awareness and involvement with what the writer considers to be a crucial moment in the thematic development of the narrative.

The voices appear to Wariinga whenever she is in a state of confusion, but on the threshold of a 'new' life. The first voice appears to Wariinga when she is about to take her life, having been fired by Boss Kihara and abandoned by 'her sweetheart, John Kimwana' (Ngugi 1982, pp. 10–13). At the door of the saloon, she sees her first vision of the Devil. Clearly, Ngugi associates the woes of Wariinga with the workings of the Devil (read the woes of capitalist Kenya). Indeed, when Wariinga is evicted from her house, the eviction is carried out by the 'Devil's Angels' (Ngugi 1982, p. 10). But for every group of the Devil's Angels there is also one single voice, one 'good Samaritan' who seeks to redeem those tormented by the Devil and its angels. At this critical moment of pain and indecision, the student leader turns out to be Wariinga's redeemer. He saves Wariinga from being hit by a car, collects her bag and waits upon her until she regains consciousness.

What Ngugi does is to appropriate the Christian notion of good and evil and use it in the explication of Wariinga's social problems. By borrowing from the Christian ethical beliefs, Ngugi hopes to appeal to the ordinary Gikuyus who are familiar with the Bible[7] while remaining steeped in the agnostic world of vice and virtue. The Devil's attempts to woo Wariinga with earthly splendours may be a raw parallel to the trials of Christ in the Bible, but the ultimate moral thrust of the trial is the triumph of vice over virtue which is at the heart of all oral tales. In spite of the apparent material gain offered by the Devil, its ultimate objective is to imprison innocent lives like that of Wariinga. The Devil thus works through materialism to entice its victims. The Devil is like the gleam, in Armah's *The Beautyful Ones Are Not Yet Born*, which imprisons all those who would move within its orbit. The voice of good on the other hand seeks to redeem the tormented souls. It is significant that after the vision of the Devil in her dreams, Wariinga comes to consciousness to listen to the voice of sanity, the voice of truth in the person of the student leader; the man who literally saves her life. At the end of the student's talk we are made aware that Wariinga has been touched positively:

> She did not understand all the things that were hinted at in the arcane language of the young man. But here and there she could sense that his words approached thoughts that she herself had had at one time. She sighed and said: 'Your words have hidden meanings. But what you say is true. These troubles have now passed beyond the limit of endurance. Who would not welcome change in order to escape from them?' (Ngugi 1982, p. 16)

It is the student leader who helps Wariinga to translate her vision into concrete reality; he guides her from a position of passivity to one of active resistance to change her situation. The student's voice seeks to influence every step that Wariinga has to take while the Devil seeks to lure her into the things that destroy the soul and body and degrade her humanity. When later in the narrative a voice confronts Wariinga after the incident at the cave and tells her that 'there is a third, a revolutionary world', it turns out that these very words were used by Muturi in Mwaura's *matatu* (Ngugi 1982, p. 184).

Wariinga's growth towards awareness is fought in the mind. Ngugi substitutes a realistic growth and development of character with the kind of mental growth that takes place after a spiritual trial – a process of soul searching that leads to clarity of vision. The clarity of vision is, of course, a product of weighing and thinking; it is the result of a delicate process of discrimination that leads to informed and democratic growth. Wariinga must learn to draw a distinction between the ways of the Devil and those of good; between the ways of the oppressor and the third voice that seeks to redeem humanity from all forms of slavery. Since much of Wariinga's woes have taken place in the past, it seems to me that Ngugi cannot readily provide for Wariinga's character transformation and so he resorts to the use of the fantastic. The Christian ethic of good versus evil lends itself to the didactic writing in which Ngugi is engaged here in order to persuade his audience to see things from a specific moral persuasion. The strength of the narrative therefore lies in the sheer weight of its moral power.

According to Ngugi, to heed the voice of the Devil is to take sides with the forces of oppression and human degradation. It is significant that when Wariinga's final trial from the Devil takes place and she is faced with the difficult choice of having to take sides with the workers, Muturi challenges her and Gatuiria to choose their side in the struggle. By the time Wariinga joins the workers at the cave, she is mentally prepared to take sides with the workers. It is at this stage that she gets a gun from Muturi; a gun which she later uses to kill the Rich Old Man. Two years later, the narrative voice tells us, Wariinga is a changed woman (Ngugi 1982, p. 215).

The voices that come to Wariinga come to her in dreams in which she is presented with both visual images and verbal communication. One of the basic usages of dreams in moralistic writing, as Kunene argues, is to use them as 'a convenient *deus ex machina* to make up for lack of convincing motivation of characters' (1989, p. 193). It seems to me that Ngugi's use of voices and dreams in *Devil on the Cross* corroborates this thesis because in the dreams the protagonist is transported into the realm of fantasy from where her soul is purged through a series of trials. The dreams therefore provide a framework for change and action on the part of the protagonist; which is not possible outside the dreams. Wariinga's dreams are essentially one-dimensional and fashioned after the biblical visions whose primary purpose was to compel the dreamer to take a specific moral position. Indeed, if it is not feasible to account for the growth and development of Wariinga from the general narrative structure, it is possible to do so through her dreams. Within the framework of characters coming to social consciousness through dreams and voices, Ngugi underscores the triumph of good over evil – the victory of forces that seek to build our humanity over those forces that seek to destroy it – but more importantly, he achieves the structural feat of character trans-formation within a simple narrative plot structure.

In *Matigari*, Ngugi weaves fantasy together with rumour. The narrator forcefully harnesses the technique of rumour-mongering in the portrayal of Matigari. The power of rumour lies in the fact that each individual is free to choose what type of information to take or leave, and also what to add to it to create a new text. Ultimately, language is manipulated to give rumour a specific angle or flavour and to generate other layers of meaning that one does not have to prove because rumour is inexhaustible – it has no end or beginning. Thus, rumour thrives in secrecy and the absence of an authentic source or primary text. Every other layer of rumour is always new and refreshing. In fact, it is the generative power of a given rumour that influences our responses or attitudes towards the rumour. 'By the time one acts in response to a rumour', Peter Amuka asserts, 'the understanding is that the very rumour has exerted its powers and yielded results and answers' (1993, p. 6). Yet rumours multiply and thrive better in a repressive society where open discourse or voices of dissent are eliminated through ideology of order.[8]

Ngugi must have been conscious of the power of rumour-mongering in Kenya when he decided to deploy this popular vehicle in his portrayal of Matigari. Rumour is such a popular and potentially subversive vehicle that President Moi is frequently compelled to warn Kenyans against rumour-mongering and to emphasise that it is treasonable.[9] Ngugi chose a vehicle that is widely accepted among his target readers and highly loathed by the Kenyan establishment. Matigari's stature as a mythical redeemer is built through rumours; the word of mouth with seamless weaves which can be stretched in all directions. He is mythologised through rumours and his identity is constructed through the rumours. He is represented by stories invented and woven around his life and adventures. When the children hurled stones at him, we read, '[n]ot even one stone touched him', and '[w]hen the stones reached him, they changed into doves' (Ngugi 1987, p. 73). The women visualise him both as 'a tiny, ordinary

looking man' and as a giant who could touch the sky
(pp. 75–6). Apparently, the women are not bothered by the
conflicting versions of Matigari's physical character. The
point is that Matigari's presence becomes a verbal conjecture
from mouth to mouth, ear to ear and of course eye to eye as
he is visualised through the language of rumours. The
rumours acquire mythical dimensions when Matigari escapes
from jail. The word goes that he brandished a flaming sword,
and the doors of jail opened. He had a voice like thunder, and
when he spoke smoke gushed from his mouth (p. 77). And at
the time of his imprisonment he is reported to have said:
'you'll see me again after three days' (p. 79). And people
believe that 'he's the one prophesied about' (p. 81).

Although Matigari himself does not claim Christ-like status,
Ngugi gives detailed circumstantial evidence that keeps the
comparison alive in the readers' minds. The fantasy of this
miracle-working redeemer is desirable, if only for its appeal to
the justice and truth that are grossly missing in the land. And
although the Matigari myth is sustainable only as a rumour,
because when the people see him they reject him, his
portrayal serves to underscore the writer–narrator's objective:
to tell and sustain a story through suspense and fantasy until
the truth about Matigari is revealed and the reader–audience
is forced to look beyond the mythical redeemer. In the end,
Matigari's rumour is incorporated into the social struggles of
the people and the rumour is wrenched from its mythology
because it has become a means of cognition; a way of understanding social processes hitherto unclear. But the myth also
turns the heat on the prophet or protagonist, because it is
only when the people have rejected Matigari that he is forced
back into the wilderness where he interprets his failure
according to the wisdom of old. Matigari's lesson is that
vision – the might of words alone – is not enough. In the
end, he returns for his guns and is ready to lay down his life
again to reclaim his house and land.

In his portrayal of Matigari, Ngugi combines rumour and
the fantasy of a redeemer after the Christian tradition, the
two forms that are contemporary and belong to a known
tradition. And by juxtaposing fantasy with the material

experience, he is able to transport Matigari and the audience from one level of experience to another: from a lower level of social awareness to a higher level of social understanding of the postcolonial absurdity. In the end Matigari gives his life to the land – again pointing to the Christ metaphor – sacrifice being the ultimate price that true patriots have to pay for the birth of a new nation. Again, the moral persuasion is keen here; it is Matigari's moral stature and what he symbolises that counts, rather than our ability to relate to him at a human level. This new moral vision is persuasively and metaphorically rendered, simply because the narrator has to carry his audience along, in the struggle for the new nation. In this new struggle, Matigari's legacy continues as symbolised in Muriuki when he unearths Matigari's weapons, but more significantly, because Matigari's rumour continued: 'Everywhere in the country the big question still remained: Who was Matigari ma Njiruungi? Was he dead, or was he alive?' (Ngugi 1987, p. 174). In real life in Kenya, Matigari's rumour as a subversive political character continued. As the author's note informs us:

> Matigari the fictional hero of the novel, was himself resurrected as a subversive political character. The novel was published in the Gikuyu language original in Kenya in October 1986. By January 1987, intelligence reports had it that peasants in Central Kenya were whispering and talking about a man called Matigari who was roaming the whole country making demands about truth and justice. There were orders for his immediate arrest, but the police discovered that Matigari was only a fictional character in a book of the same name. (p. viii)

Evidently, this is a good instance of a literary text – a written text – entering both oral and contemporary political discourse. As an intervention in Kenya's oral discourse, *Matigari* was now open to new layers of meaning through rumour and the spoken word. The text was throwing up new and seamless oral narratives and in the process turning a fictional hero into a subversive political character. Yet, Ngugi's later narratives written in Gikuyu still occupy an ambiguous literary space in spite of Ngugi's attempt to mythologise his own hero, Matigari, as reflected in the statement above. The readership still remains a literate, distant audience and not necessarily the peasantry and the workers that Ngugi has in mind as his target audience. A survey carried out by Ngugi's publisher, Henry Chakava (1993, p. 73), shows that the two novels in Gikuyu have attracted very limited readership and there is no guarantee that the limited readership reflected through the sales comes from the workers and peasants.[10]

Ngugi's Achievement

Within the framework of the popular genre, however, one can conclude that Ngugi is able to transform our traditional understanding of character in the novel by drawing our attention to the story – the central discourse in the narratives – thereby moving away from the traditional notions of character delineation. The use of popular forms has enabled him to provide motivation for his characters' actions and to effect their social transformation: if not always convincingly, still within a simple plot structure. In a way, Ngugi validates Barthes's theoretical supposition that characters are in fact mere tropes in the narrative (Barthes 1974, pp. 178–9). To this extent Ngugi is challenging the traditional notions of complex characters as the hallmark of a good narrative. He attaches great value to the story and to how the same narrative could be rendered persuasively in the postcolonial narratives originally written in Gikuyu. Thus, elements that are traditionally considered central to the novel form, such as credibility of character and complexity of plot structure, are inevitably subordinated to the dominant discourse in his narratives – the absurd drama of the postcolonial state in Kenya. However, Ngugi's characters remain mechanical allegorical symbols; they are mere signs that draw our attention to Ngugi's sense of Kenyan history and not to other competing versions of the nation's history and the politics which underpin its multifaceted layers.

5

Allegory, Romance and the Nation: Women as Allegorical Figures in Ngugi's Novels

Romantic Relationships as Allegorical Tropes

Ngugi uses allegory in most of his works to explore romantic relationships as symbolic representations of what takes place in the wider society. One of the most intriguing features of Ngugi's writing is the way he places the female protagonists in romantic relationships which readily pass for allegorical tropes. Romantic relationships form a recurring subject in virtually all Ngugi's works. His female archetypes are quite similar to the extent that they become sites for contesting the desired nation.

In his earlier texts the portrayal of women owes something to a long-standing iconography of women in nationalist literature which inevitably mobilises women as the central metaphor for the nation. Ngugi's women protagonists in these novels fulfil something of this function by becoming primary sites for testing the reconciliation of ethnicity and the nation, tradition and modernity, betrayal and hope and, indeed, the possibility of rebirth. In the latter texts, however, the women protagonists become an index, a reflection of the state of the nation. In their portrayal they often stand for the state of degradation in a postcolony and in their striving gesture towards the possibilities of redemption and the birth of a nation free of class exploitation in the first instance and free of gender inequality in the second. In other words, if Ngugi enlists women as carriers of tradition and nationalism in his earlier texts, in his later texts he mobilises them as metaphors of a class war.

The Portrayal of Women in the Earlier Novels

In Chapter 2 I mentioned that one of the basic concerns of Ngugi in his earlier narratives is his attempt to reconcile the apparent contradiction between ethnicity and nationalism. The tensions associated with ethnicity and its meaning are, as we have already noted, numerous. Ethnicity must bear the weight of being ossified and backward-looking, it must also refract a sentimentalised construction of precolonial society as an organic whole. And, finally, ethnicity in certain parts must stand for itself and the nation simultaneously. The strand of investing the 'tribe' with the nation is perhaps not pronounced but is mediated obliquely through the Gikuyu myth of origin as we saw in Chapter 4. Significantly, the portrayal of the tribe as an organic whole and Ngugi's gesture towards a reconciled nationhood are mediated by women. In *The River Between* women are the repositories of ethnicity. Miriamu, Joshua's wife, despite her Christianity is seen as essentially Gikuyu: 'one could still tell by her eyes that this was a religion learnt and accepted; inside the true Gikuyu woman was sleeping' (Ngugi 1965, p. 34). And although Muthoni's death is meant to gesture towards the possibility of reconciling the traditional ways of the 'tribe' and Western culture in the form of Christianity, Muthoni's body remains a site upon which the purity of the tribe is encoded. When Muthoni tells Waiyaki that '[she] want[s] to be a woman made beautiful in the ways of the tribe' (p. 44), she is confirming her role as the custodian of tradition and purity of the community. Womanhood here acts as the buffer zone for ethnicity and the implied 'fixed' identity of the tribe which is crystallised in female circumcision. Ngotho's wives in *Weep Not, Child* also seem to have no voice and have learnt to live in harmony within an obviously acrimonious polygamous structure. Like Miriamu and Muthoni, they cling to the ways of the tribe passively and uphold the patriarchal structure unchallenged.

If the burden of carrying the ethnic agenda rests with Muthoni, Ngugi resorts to a romantic affair between Waiyaki and Nyambura to articulate nationalism as the ultimate alternative to ethnicity. Although Waiyaki's private inclinations are particularised in this romantic love, which is posed as mutually exclusive to public commitment, the romance is undoubtedly Ngugi's vehicle for the ideal nationhood. Just when the themes of reconciliation and unity seem to be fading, they are replaced by the theme of romance as a trope for achieving communal redemption. Where the rhetorics of modern nationalism such as education, unity and reconciliation have failed, Ngugi inserts romance. Significantly, it is only after the relationship with Nyambura is established and made public that Waiyaki is able to articulate, even if only in very general terms, the nature of his mission: 'all at once Waiyaki realized what the ridges wanted. People wanted action now. Now he knew what he would preach if he ever got another chance: education for unity. Unity for political freedom' (Ngugi 1965, p. 143).

The use of romance as a figure for the ideal nationhood is also captured in the relationship between Njoroge and Mwihaki in *Weep Not, Child*. The young Mwihaki and Njoroge, caught between their warring families, represent in their romance the possibility of unity and reconciliation threatened by the Mau Mau war. Mwihaki's father, Jacobo, is a homeguard fighting on the side of the colonial government and Njoroge's father is an *ahoi* whose sons have been enlisted in the Mau Mau resistance to the colonial regime. Thus the moral dilemma facing the fighting sides and the tragedy that seems to threaten the Agikuyu community and by implication the imagined Kenyan nation is encapsulated in this tragic romantic affair. Tragic because this innocent love, symbolic of the nascent Kenyan nation-state growing out of the womb of colonial experience, is shattered by the violence of the emergency period. Ngugi seems to have been so keen on the disruptive nature of the emergency that he picks up this theme again in *A Grain of Wheat*. The conditions of the emergency almost disrupt the love and marriage between Gikonyo and Mumbi. Detained for his part in the struggle, Gikonyo capitulates to the authorities because he wants to come back to Mumbi. When he returns, he discovers that Mumbi has had a child with Karanja and he is distraught. In a major development to the sequel of romances in his first two novels, Ngugi transforms this romantic relationship that is fraught with tragedy into a symbol of regeneration, hope and reconciliation. In the end Gikonyo is carving a stool for Mumbi and Mumbi is expecting Gikonyo's child. Their recent self-rediscovery in forgiveness and reconciliation lifts the burden of guilt from their hearts and shoulders and they are used to point to the possibility of renewal and the birth of a new nation. As characters whose names echo those of the founders of the Gikuyu nation, Gikonyo (Gikuyu) and Mumbi stand for change in permanence and hope in the future of the community. Their romance also anticipates the struggles and triumphs that Wanja of *Petals of Blood* goes through in the postcolonial state. In a significant sense, romance and the trials of womanhood in *A Grain of Wheat* act as major indicators of the things to come; they herald Ngugi's transition from nationalist rhetorics to the radical class perspective that we encounter in his later texts. This radical shift is most evident in Ngugi's choice of female protagonists who are invariably drawn from the marginalised groups within the society. The female protagonist in Ngugi's later novels is either from a peasant or working-class background, made pregnant by a wealthy old man who destroys her life and later rejects her. They include Beatrice in 'Minutes of Glory' (*Secret Lives*), Wanja in *Petals of Blood*, Wariinga in *Devil on the Cross*, and Guthera in *Matigari*.

Romance and the Portrayal of Women in the Later Novels

If class perspective remains the ideological hallmark of Ngugi's later novels, this ideological shift is best captured in the romantic relationships that have remained a major feature of his later novels. On the one hand, we have those relationships that express what Ngugi considers to be the impossibility of romantic affairs between rich and poor, elite and working class; and on the other, we have those relationships that offer the working class the possibility of harmonising or consummating the interests of marginalised groups within society. In these two types of relationships Ngugi explores the antagonism, which he shows as irreconcilable, between the oppressor and the oppressed, and the possibility of patriotism among the workers in their struggle to realise the ideal nation. The affairs of Wanja–Kimeria, Wariinga–Gatuiria, and Matigari–Guthera, are presented as different kinds of romantic tropes.

Wanja is depicted as a young schoolgirl who falls victim to a wealthy former homeguard, Kimeria, who seduces her with gifts, confuses her and makes her pregnant. When Kimeria fails to marry her, she escapes from home and becomes a barmaid. Wariinga, in *Devil on the Cross*, is also a schoolgirl who becomes a victim of the Rich Old Man, and as a secretary to Boss Kihara she is sexually harassed by him. She is also let down by her university boyfriend, and at the end of the narrative she is abandoned by Gatuiria. One meets similar failed romantic relationships in Ngugi's *I Will Marry When I Want*. Here the marriage between the poor Kigunda's daughter, Gathoni, and John Muhuuni, the son of the wealthy Kioi, cannot succeed because of the socioeconomic differences between the two families.

All the relationships above have similar features. In each case we have a situation in which the rich and propertied elite attempts to take advantage of poor women. We have relationships characterised by exploitation and hypocrisy. The rich men turn the poor women into sexual objects for male pleasure and the elite men cannot commit themselves to genuine relationships with the poor women. Thus, Kimeria and Gitahi, by taking advantage of Wanja and Wariinga respectively, destroy their futures. Similarly, the educated elite represented by Gatuiria and the university student both let Wariinga down at her most critical hours of need. Here Ngugi pushes us to read romantic intrigues as metaphoric parallels to social relations in the society. Romantic relationships between the rich and the poor, Ngugi would seem to suggest, have no social legitimacy and are doomed from the start by the antagonistic and contradictory relations of exploitation between these two broad social groups. The vacillating elite are also caught up within these failed relationships and tragically find themselves torn between their class interests and the interests of the marginalised groups with whom they enter into relationships. Thus the working class and the propertied cannot have a viable relationship without conflict and tragedy, in the same way that these two classes cannot forge a mutually beneficial economic relationship in social life. Thus, the characters involved in these relationships are portrayed in such a way that they become social symbols;

they become illustrative figures of broad social relationships within Kenyan society.

The type of romantic relationship described here is contrasted with a relationship in which we have a metaphoric parallelism between passion and patriotism, such as the relationship between Guthera and Matigari. Like Wariinga, Guthera's father was a patriot who supported the liberation struggle. Guthera's father 'was found carrying bullets in his Bible' and he was killed by the colonial government, leaving Guthera and the other children destitute (Ngugi 1982, pp. 35–6). She is portrayed as a morally upright girl who refuses to yield to the sexual demands of a police superintendent to get her father released from prison. Finally, it is economic deprivation which drives her to prostitution. Guthera is initiated into the struggle when she breaks her vow that she would never give her body to any policeman; she sleeps with a prison guard in order to help Matigari escape. But perhaps more importantly, just before the climax of the narrative, she subordinates herself to Matigari – the 'noble patriarch' – in a symbolic marital union of comrades, with Muriuki as their adopted child. It is apparent here that Matigari behaves like a patriarch, and Guthera in her joyful submission to him merely serves to reinforce the popular image of women as docile – ironically, the very image Ngugi seems to be fighting in all his narratives. The union between Matigari and Guthera is contrived and simplistic and it does not enhance the thematic concerns of the narrative, but rather undermines the well-known image of Ngugi's characters as all-powerful and resourceful.

In their romantic relationship, Guthera and Matigari find common ground in their background of poverty, in their common goal never to prostitute their bodies for the oppressor's money and in their common vision to liberate their society. Every obstacle that the lovers encounter heightens not only their mutual desire to be a couple, it also heightens their love for the potential nation in which the affair could be consummated. It would seem to me that this is the ideal romantic relationship, according to Ngugi, a romantic relationship which becomes a celebration of the ideal nation's hope.

We encounter a similar relationship between Wanja and Abdulla which, as Stratton writes, 'signifies the regeneration of potency in the struggle for freedom from oppression and exploitation in present-day Kenya' (1994, p. 50). Stratton continues to assert that Wanja's pregnancy, 'preceded by an act of infanticide on the eve of independence and followed by years of barrenness – is the promise of the rebirth of the nation' (p. 50). It is a relationship that parallels patriotism because it is based on mutual class interests and hostility to those forces that seek to exploit and degrade man and woman. Thus, real passion, for Ngugi, would seem to parallel patriotism; and the consummation of a romantic relationship as a marriage is a symbolic celebration of the ideal nation still subterranean – the 'kingdom of man and woman ... joying and loving in creative labour' (Ngugi 1977, p. 344).

However, the reappearance of similar female characters in different novels suggests that Ngugi has a formula regarding the exploitation of women. For example, he would have us believe that it is only the wealthy bourgeois class that exploits and oppresses women from the worker and peasant classes, while working-class or peasant men never exploit women. A critical analysis of Wanja's portrayal serves as a good illustration of Ngugi's contradictions on feminist discourses in Kenya and as a way of examining the male-bourgeois domination and capitalist entrapment of Ngugi's heroines.

The Problem of Women as Victims: Wanja in *Petals of Blood*

The significance of Wanja lies in the fact that she expresses Ngugi's ambivalent position on feminist discourses in Kenya. On the one hand, Ngugi portrays Wanja as a woman who transcends traditional limitations and, on the other hand, she is portrayed as the victim of colonial capitalist society.

For example, as a primary school pupil, Wanja was referred to as Wanja Kahii (a boy) and she is good in things which are considered to fall specifically within the male domain such as freewheeling, tree-climbing and maths. Wanja's apparent disposition to 'masculine' values is not explored fully by Ngugi to shed light on gender relations within traditional

Gikuyu society and instead there seems to be an unspoken approval, at least from the narrative point of view, that certain things belong to the domain of men. A woman like Wanja who can do the things assigned by society to men is seen as unique and, in a sense, naturally predisposed to subverting gender stereotypes. The narrative is silent on the impact of patriarchy which socialises both men and women to accept certain roles in society as gender-determined. To imply – as the narrative does – that to be liberated a woman must struggle for the so-called 'male' subjects like mathematics, in the case of Wanja, and engineering, in the case of Wariinga in *Devil on the Cross*, is an oversimplification of gender discrimination and the process of mental liberation that it requires. Wariinga's fantasy and change may be credible given her past experiences, but her dramatic trans-formation into an engineer, independent and contented in her new social role, is most incredible. Ngugi is totally oblivious to the possible social constraints that frustrate most women and young Kenyans from acquiring formal education and taking up meaningful careers. According to Ngugi all that is needed is the willpower and the natural zeal to conquer 'the Devil's empire' which is the male-dominated capitalist world – and all shall be added unto you. What Ngugi does is thus to reverse or simply convert 'stereotypical feminine qualities into equally stereotypical masculine ones' (Stratton 1994, p. 162). The point is that women's liberation requires more than just the acquisition of masculine values, even with the best intentions on the part of the writer.

Women can still enter all the male-dominated areas and still remain entrapped within the male-constructed identity of women as mere objects of sex and as naturally inferior. Wanja, in spite of her strength and success as a woman, still considers her sexual organs as a curse – a source of slavery: 'If you have a cunt ... if you are born with this hole, instead of it being a source of pride, you are doomed to either marrying someone or else being a whore. You eat or you are eaten' (Ngugi 1977, p. 293).

Evidently, Wanja is confusing issues here, because it is not so much the possession of the 'cunt' in itself that enslaves her, but rather the social attitudes that the society attaches to womanhood and the construction of women's identity as the weaker sex and therefore the object of male sexual gratification. For all her power and strength, Wanja is still objectified by Ngugi and often portrayed as having that irresistible charm that is needed to seduce men.

The dominant image of Wanja that emerges in the narrative is that of a victim of male bourgeois domination and capitalist forces engendered by colonialism. We have already seen that her exploitation by a wealthy former homeguard, Mr Kimeria, drives her to prostitution in the first instance. She tells Munira of how she had no choice but to become a bar-attendant – a job description which is synonymous with prostitution in Kenya.

When Wanja finds city life difficult, she runs back to Ilmorog to join her grandmother in the hope that she can start the kind of life where she could earn a decent living and at the same time be useful to others. But the combined blow of her grandmother's death, Karega's escape and the advent of the new economic and social order in Ilmorog sends Wanja back to whoredom. This time round, Wanja has acquired a new dictum – 'Eat or you are eaten' (Ngugi 1977, p. 293). Significantly, Wanja becomes a victim of local capitalists acting in conjunction with international capital in Ilmorog. She is forced to sell their house to Mzigo and she cannot continue with her grandmother's business because the licence has been cancelled and subsequently awarded to the multinationals. Through his depiction of Wanja's trials, the writer attempts to make us appreciate the forces that send Wanja to prostitution.

Ngugi would want to portray Wanja as a typical reflection of the material conditions of the exploited majority of women in Kenya. Wanja shows the upward mobility of only a select few to the top levels of the economic and social echelons, made possible through prostitution. For Wanja to rise she is forced not just to 'prostitute' her body, but also to put those of other women into her service. Thus, for Ngugi, prostitution becomes a symbol of degradation rather than liberty.[1] Ngugi sees it as a path to entrapment and slavery. But as Luise White (1990) has shown, women sometimes seized niches in the expanding and poorly organised urban economy, as prostitutes and landlords, providing essential services to male migrant labourers. But more importantly, White's study also brings out the basic ambiguity in colonial relationships in which the women were both subverting the cultural project of colonialism and subsidising the economic one. This ambiguity is best captured in Wanja's character, although the writer ultimately condemns her for prostitution. She was able to seize niches within the nascent capitalist economy, while subverting the colonial enterprise through her social networks with her call-girls, and her relationships with the working-class leaders and the African shareholders in the new capital engendered by colonialism. And although prostitution is portrayed as a degrading occupation, it is the main source of capital accumulation available to women in the postcolonial state. 'What is the difference whether you are sweating it out on a plantation, in a factory or lying on your back, anyway?', Wanja asks (Ngugi 1977, p. 293). Prostitution is thus presented, at another level, as an indicator of the state of the nation in Kenya. Kenya's position of dependency in the world economy is likened to prostitution as a social institution. It is a mirror to the economic prostitution of postcolonial Kenya. As Karega – the hero of *Petals of Blood* – asserts, 'a man who has never set foot on this land can sit in a New York or London office and determine what I shall eat, read, think, do only because he sits on a heap of billions'. 'In such a world,' Karega tells Munira, 'we are all prostituted' (p. 240). Thus, postcolonial Kenya is represented as a country in a state of degradation. And as Stratton rightly argues, Wanja is the 'index of the state of the nation' (1994, p. 48) because she represents the nation's moments of degradation in her portrait as abused womanhood and an allegorical parallel to the postcolonial state in Kenya.

Ngugi depicts Wanja as a victim and as subject to some kind of cast-iron fate. On the march to the city she meets Kimeria who corrupted her in her youth and the same Kimeria becomes one of the black directors of Theng'eta Breweries. As Wanja herself observes:

> I could hardly accept this twist of fate ... Kimeria, who had ruined my life and later humiliated me by making me sleep with him during our journey to the city ... this same

Kimeria was one of those who would benefit from the new economic progress of Ilmorog. (Ngugi 1977, p. 293)

Wherever Wanja turns she is confronted by her destroyers. And although in the new Ilmorog she becomes larger than life – fabled as the founder of the town – she remains a victim trapped in a vicious circle from which there is very little hope of escape. In an interview with Anita Shreve, Ngugi emphasises the entrapment of Wanja in the system. 'There are always possibilities of renewal and growth', he says of Wanja; '[b]ut', he adds, 'only in a different kind of system' (Shreve 1977, p. 36).

Ultimately, Ngugi, without saying so, succumbs to the traditional male stereotypical image of the prostitute woman as degenerate and immoral. The narrative voice calls prostitution 'a career of always being trodden upon, a career of endless shame and degeneration' (Ngugi 1977, p. 329). This is what Karega is getting at when he refers disparagingly to Wanja's way of dealing with her predicament as a form of 'static vision' and as perverted worship of a degraded 'world in which one could only be clean by wiping his dirt and shit and urine on others' (p. 303).

Ngugi is moralising the issue by questioning Wanja's prostitution as a method to free herself and ultimately he rejects the possibility of any form of struggle within the limits of a repressive patriarchal society. We feel for Wanja when the 'morally upright' Karega condemns her and, in anguish, she dismisses his ideological arrogance by telling him that she too has tried to fight her exploiters in the only way she can, and that is by using her sexual powers (Ngugi 1977, p. 327). The implied ideological position that women must wait for their liberty in the 'kingdom of man and woman' (p. 344) is both simplistic and idealistic as it privileges class struggle over gender issues. For Ngugi, the ultimate moral test is the side one takes in a class war, and since Wanja has not taken sides with the struggling masses, the prostitutes and the workers, she is condemned to capitalist doom. There is no doubt that Ngugi shares in Munira's puritan attitude towards Wanja. According to Munira, Wanja as a prostitute is a symbol of 'Jezebel' (p. 332) and it is significant that the so-called change that takes place in Wanja comes after the burning of Wanja's whorehouse by Munira. Ngugi's moral purging leads logically to political activism on the side of the oppressed. And accordingly, it is not until Wanja decides to take a stand in the struggle that we are made to understand that she begins to feel 'the stirrings of a new person' (p. 328). She decides to give up prostitution and she falls pregnant. If prostitution is allegorical of the decadent state of the nation, then motherhood is allegorical of national rebirth and regeneration: 'the movement of the springs of life ... the world' (p. 315).

Although Ngugi's use of the image of the prostitute for the character of the most liberated woman in the novel is significant, it raises a number of contentious issues in gender studies that Ngugi fails to resolve. The first such issue is the debate over the role of colonialism and in turn the capitalist system in the liberation of women. The second issue is whether prostitution offers women any form of liberation within a patriarchal society, and ultimately what the prostitute's identity means to one's material position in Kenya.

From Ngugi's portrayal of Wanja one is tempted to conclude that colonialism both empowered and disempowered women. The development of capitalism in Ilmorog makes it possible for Wanja to free herself from male domination to the extent that the new Ilmorog provides scope for unconventional female behaviour and the nascent capitalist forces permit a degree of female economic independence. Wanja becomes a prostitute as a means to fight male domination and the system, something she could not have done in the traditional context. And yet Ngugi's insistence that Wanja's ultimate move to large-scale prostitution is some form of degeneration and entrapment can only serve to expose his ambivalent attitude towards the stereotype of the degenerate prostitute that is often found in African literature.

Ngugi's portrayal of the character of Wanja is even more disturbing because Ngugi has loaded too many traits on this one character and failed to reconcile all these traits within the narrative in a credible manner. Wanja represents too many types of women at once. She is the schoolgirl ravished by a sugar-daddy, a barmaid, a prostitute in various forms, a businesswoman, a visionary and at times she represents the peasant woman. If we examine even the dialogue Ngugi gives Wanja we find her a 'complex' character. When, for example, she states that 'we all carry maimed souls and we are looking for a cure' (Ngugi 1977, p. 73), we ask ourselves in what language a barmaid would be making such a profound statement. The whole novel and the other characters appear to revolve around Wanja and she has had an affair with virtually all the male characters in the narrative: Karega, Munira, Abdulla, Kimeria, Chui and Mzigo.

Wanja's vision and awareness of the forces that lead her into prostitution and her practice are contradictory from the point of view of the narrative. Her understanding of the destruction and exploitation of poor women under capitalism seems to concur with that of the author. Wanja's argument that there is no 'difference whether you are sweating it out on a plantation, in a factory or lying on your back' would seem to tally with Ngugi's position that sexual exploitation of women is not any different from the exploitation of workers in factories or plantations; they are all victims of capitalism. Wanja, however, seems to suggest that women are doomed to exploitation because of their sex. And yet she becomes a manipulator and lives off the bodies of other women. The writer seems to be interested more in using her to illustrate his thesis on the exploitation of women in the postcolonial state, than in using Wanja's experiences as a study into the position of women at a specific historical juncture in Kenya. Wanja herself conceives of her life in images of entrapment: 'She decided that maybe everything was simply a matter of love and hate. Love and hate – Siamese twins – back to back in a human heart. Because you loved you also hated' (Ngugi 1977, p. 335).

Wanja's 'liberation' or conversion to the struggle is sudden and it comes after a self-righteous ideological diatribe from Karega who accuses her of complicity with the system of destruction. The sudden change, however, does not help Wanja to come to terms with her predicament – her entrapment – as a woman. Instead, Wanja is guilty because she has been an exploiter – a woman who has lived off the blood of other women and abused her own body in capital gain. She has been a traitor to the struggle of the oppressed. All her tragic life would seem to count for nothing, but a bizarre attempt to abdicate her moral and political responsibility. We are made to understand that she had undergone an abortion after falling pregnant as a schoolgirl and she is still haunted by guilt. Politically, she has succumbed to the values of capitalist exploitation instead of throwing in her lot with the people's struggle in Ilmorog and is, therefore, a traitor.

When Wanja's final salvation comes, it is through the mystery of fire which remains a dubious motif in her life. In the end her change is clouded with fear, mystery and lack of a conviction that comes out of clear understanding – even in Ngugi's materialist terms. And yet we are told that in her moment of reawakening 'she felt the stirrings of a new person ... She had after all been baptized by fire' (Ngugi 1977, p. 337). For Ngugi, fire is a purifying force, a strengthening force. Munira refers to Wanja as the mythical Phoenix bird that is reborn after fire. Munira himself believes in this purifying force of fire. After his first sexual encounter with a woman he burns an imitation of the woman's house after which 'he felt truly purified by fire' (p. 14). Fire here has an abstract ethereal quality to it. It is a mysterious power whose effects are not visible but are felt inwardly by Munira and Wanja.

Fire, in *Petals of Blood*, is also seen as an agent of destruction. And yet, even on this level the destruction by fire is connected to the idea of sin and punishment. Wanja's first house is burnt down by 'tribal' chauvinists who do not want her to have an affair with her Somalian lover. Munira seeks to destroy Wanja's house because to him she is evil. When her house is finally burnt down, Munira is thrilled that God's will has been accomplished. The four directors of Theng'eta Breweries meet their deaths through fire, again apparently for the sins they have committed against the people of Ilmorog, the Kenyan people.

Wanja is haunted by fire on both levels. She is terrified of fire yet at the same time attracted to its 'cleansing' power. Her aunt, a freedom fighter, was destroyed by fire. With these two levels of fire in *Petals of Blood* Ngugi is suggesting that

Wanja needed purification and, if so, from what does she need purification? And if it involves punishment, for what was she being punished? Wanja's own words on the burning of her aunt do not make the mystery any clearer:

> I have liked to believe that she burnt herself like Buddhists do, which then makes me think of the water and the fire of the second coming to cleanse and bring purity to our earth of cruelty and loneliness ... (Ngugi 1977, p. 65)

In the same paragraph, Wanja talks of her desire to set herself on fire with the aim of purifying herself.

Ngugi is obviously trapped in the Christian moral vision that he has appropriated to explain the nature of the capitalist world. This moral stance also agrees with his epistemological outlook and historical sense, which defines people in terms of good and evil, patriots and traitors, fighters and liberators. At a symbolic level then, Wanja has to purge herself from her immoral past and a past of political betrayal. Only then can she be liberated. This process of purification ought to lead her to take sides with the oppressed in the battle to usher in a new social order, 'bringing to an end the reign of the few over the many ... Then, only then, would the kingdom of man and woman really begin' (Ngugi 1977, p. 344).

Ngugi's position lends itself to moralising. For Ngugi, there is no borderline between personal morality and political engagement. It is one's involvement in the political struggle that defines one's moral position. Wanja's moral integrity can only be realised within the context of class struggle for justice and equality. No other struggles exist outside class war. This logically leads to an ideological absolutism in which other forms of democratic struggles are repressed in favour of rigid class parameters as the only litmus test for change within society. No democratic spaces exist for women outside class struggle. As a result Wanja loses the more human and personal conflicts that we tend to associate with characters who represent an historical moment.

The image of the prostitute is a cypher for the evils of colonial and postcolonial capitalism in Ngugi's narrative. The modern capitalist system enslaves women and compounds their domination by men. In Ngugi's view the acquisitive spirit of capitalism twists the relationship between man and woman into a relationship of ownership and domination.

Conclusion

I have argued that although Ngugi is sympathetic to women as subjects of oppression, he is primarily interested in women as exploited workers or producers. He shows little interest in the constraints placed on women by patriarchy and religion, for example. Ngugi's women are basically victims of capitalist male-bourgeois domination. Their exploitation is therefore not very different from that suffered by the oppressed male and this tends to obscure the interaction between gender and other social institutions that a whole 'clan' of women may suffer from in spite of their class background. It also creates the impression that there are no essential differences between working-class women; let alone implying the view that working-class men do not oppress women.

Although Ngugi displays the awareness that Kenyan women are subject to double oppression both as women and as workers he tends to suggest that what is urgent is the liberation of women as workers rather than women *qua* women. This position tends to obscure a number of issues. For example, by reducing the oppression of women to that of class interest, Ngugi tends to gloss over patriarchal issues. He is silent on the socialisation of women that prepares them to accept their inferior status and ignores the subordination of women in precolonial Kenya. Ngugi would seem to imply that female exploitation is essentially a colonial evil; indeed, that the status of women only worsened with the advent of capitalism in Africa. It is for this reason that the struggle for women's liberation remains, for Ngugi, a class war against imperialism. It is also not surprising that Ngugi is silent on women's domestic struggles – the struggle within the home. By overlooking this area, he privileges political struggle over and above other forms of social struggles that women are engaged in. It is clear that, for him, the domination and exploitation of women can be conceived of only in class terms. Ngugi seems to suggest that women, together with the male working class, should fight for the freedom of all by working towards the dismantling of the oppressive capitalist structure.

6

Ngugi's Portrayal of the Community, Heroes and the Oppressed

Narrating the Community and the Elite in Ngugi's Earlier Novels

One of the most striking features of Ngugi's narrative over the years is the central role that the elite play within it. In virtually all his novels, Ngugi constitutes the educated elite as the shapers of the new nation-state and its modernist ideology, whether this ideology is rooted in the emergent nationalist discourses of his earlier novels or in the radical socialist vision of his later novels. It is safe to argue that the educated elite play a mediating role between the colonial structures and quest for freedom, between the neocolonial structures and the struggles of the people for a new social order. It is this role as brokers of the modernist ideology that shapes the imagination of protonationalists, like Waiyaki, and forms the basis of the anticolonial struggle in *Weep Not, Child* and Kihika's call for national sacrifice in *A Grain of Wheat*. In *The River Between*, Waiyaki's heroism is celebrated and the emphasis is on his estrangement from the community. His role as a mediator between the antagonistic groups in his community becomes both his source of power and marginalisation – and indeed Ngugi's expression of the ambivalence which characterises nationalism.

The position of Waiyaki in the text as a mediator seems to tally with the ambiguous role of the elite within the decolonisation project in Africa. As we saw in the introductory chapter, restoration of the community to itself is a precondition for the processes that culminate in the building of a nation. And, as Stuart Hall argues, nations are symbolic communities whose full materialisation depends on the ability to weave together a narrative that will win the sympathy of the intended subjects (Hall *et al.* 1992). This is precisely what Ngugi seeks to do through Waiyaki: that is, to create a nationalist discourse through the creation of independent schools around which the Gikuyu people would be mobilised as a unitary community. Ngugi says that, 'in the novel itself there is physically a river between two hills that house two communities which keep quarrelling but I maintain, you know, that the river between can be a factor which brings people together as well as being a factor of separation. It can both unite and separate' (cited in Duerden and Pieterse 1972, p. 125). It is Waiyaki who encapsulates the possibility of this unity in his role as a political broker of the modernist nationalist project that Ngugi desires for his people. Edward Said has argued that in *The River Between* Ngugi rewrites the colonialist discourse 'by inducing life into Conrad's river [in *The Heart of Darkness*] on the very first page' (Said 1994, p. 254) of *The River Between*:

> The River was called Honia, which meant cure, or bring-back-to-life. Honia river never dried: it seemed to possess a strong will to live, scorning droughts and weather changes. And it went on in the very same way, never hurrying, never hesitating. People saw this and they were happy. (Ngugi 1965, p. 1)

Whatever the limitations of Waiyaki, he stands for the new mythos that Ngugi seeks to generate in order to heal and restore the community to itself. Waiyaki's separatist education is one of the very first attempts to legitimise anti-colonial discourse in Ngugi's narrative. It was, in a way, in spite of the contradictions I raised earlier, a major attempt to wrest the discursive space from the coloniser and to restore agency of sorts to the colonised subjects. For them, this was only possible through a forging of a sense of community among the Africans, the struggle for unity which was at the heart of most nationalist discourses. And yet one cannot help but notice the moral dilemma that confronts Waiyaki as the 'nation builder'. The dilemma that Waiyaki faces is homologous to Ngugi's own class position as a member of the Kenyan elite at the time of the text's writing in the early 1960s. Waiyaki's choice to distance himself from the Kiama, a movement which was struggling for land, and in its place push for political emancipation through education, has a great deal to do with the ambivalence of the Kenyan elite towards the Mau Mau that the Kiama represents in the text.

Soon after Kenya's independence the majority of the Kenyan elite, chiefly represented by Kenyatta, saw the Mau Mau as a discredited organisation whose role in the struggle for independence had to be repressed. After all, the Kenya African National Union (KANU) leadership was openly calling for people to forget the past, eschew violence and rally behind Kenyatta, who was increasingly beginning to replace the Mau Mau as the central force behind Kenya's independence. It is Kenyatta's detention and sacrifice that was constantly emphasised. Just a year before Kenya's independence, Kenyatta had warned: 'We are determined to have independence in peace, and we shall not allow hooligans to rule Kenya. We must have no hatred towards one another. Mau Mau was a disease which had been eradicated, and must never be remembered again' (Kenyatta 1968, p. 189). Strong words to come from a leader who was seen as the main source of inspiration for the freedom fighters, and yet this was the popular line taken by a broad section of the Kenyan elite in the period leading to independence and after. Although it seems unlikely that Ngugi would have displayed similar sentiments and loathing for the Mau Mau, his portrayal of Waiyaki and his position in relation to the warring factions in the text speak to the nationalist agenda of the time. Ian Glenn is therefore right in saying:

> Waiyaki's relationship to the Kiama is marked by ambivalences that recall Kenyatta's to the Mau Mau: he is the source of its strength, distances himself from it haphazardly, and is innocent of its violent intentions. Though he realises the justice of their claims and concerns, his version of the correct method of political emancipation is that of education for unity. (Glenn 1981, p. 55)

The point being made here is that the elite positioned themselves as the brokers of Kenya's nationalist agenda and national unity was being erected as a repudiation of anything that would threaten this agenda. Buitenhuijs is therefore right, in part, in saying that the need for national unity and reconciliation between the Mau Mau fighters and the loyalists influenced the post-independence attitude towards the Mau Mau (1973, pp. 50–9). To privilege the role played by the Mau Mau fighters would have been tantamount to suggesting that only the Gikuyu, and indeed only a small section of the Gikuyu, fought for independence, a position that would have alienated those ethnic groups not involved in the armed struggle. Kenyatta positioned himself as the ultimate archi-tecture of this national unity: 'The most essential need which I have constantly sought to proclaim and fulfil in Kenya has been that of national unity; nationhood and familyhood must and can be contrived out of our many tribes and cultures' (Kenyatta 1968, p. ix). Ngugi, too, as I have argued in the introductory chapter, was grappling with the issues of ethnicity and nationalism. 'To look from the tribe to a wider concept of human association is to be progressive. When this begins to happen, a Kenya nation will be born' (Ngugi 1972, p. 24). Ngugi wrote these words in his collection of essays which have been read as an integral part of the fictional world of *The River Between*, *Weep Not, Child* and *A Grain of Wheat*. Significantly, Ngugi's article was entitled, 'Kenya: The Two Rifts', a title reminiscent of the title and issues raised in *The River Between* in particular. Clearly, Ngugi, like many of his peers in the early 1960s, saw nation-building as the fundamental mission of the elite at the time. But it was a mission that was fraught with contradictions and ambiguities that Ngugi had to distance himself from in his later works. One such contradiction was the orchestrated attempt within the mainstream politics in Kenya to downplay the heroic role of the Mau Mau and to replace it with the Kenyatta myth 'as the sole, single-handed fighter for Kenya's independence' (Ngugi 1981a, p. 89), that Maughan-Brown (1985) has written about so eloquently. It seems to me that the celebration of Waiyaki, his tensions and uncertainties when it comes to the place of the Kiama in the anticolonial struggle, must be located in the ambivalent sociopolitical climate in Kenya in the 1960s when *The River Between* was written. As Ian Glenn has suggested, the nationalist perspective privileged in the text points to 'the problems Ngugi faced: how to produce a "nation-building" text that would do justice to all, but primarily suggest, as K. A. N. U. was suggesting, that the valid choice is through unity and education rather than violence aimed at restitution of the land' (Glenn 1981, p. 55).

The ambivalence towards the Mau Mau war and the violence associated with it persists in *Weep Not, Child.* Once again the politics of the day are mediated through the eyes of Njoroge who embodies the aspirations of the elite and cherishes the ideals of unity that transcend both racial and ethnic barriers. And yet in this text Ngugi is painfully aware of the impossibility of reconciliation due to the repressive colonial structures that have driven the youth into the forest. It is the same repressive structures that destroy Ngugi's young, but naive hero, driven gradually towards self-destruction. In the circumstances, Ngugi seems to be suggesting that the nationalist dream is but an illusion. The community cannot reconstitute itself purely on the basis of a modernist vision such as Njoroge's who, like Waiyaki before him, privileges education over land restitution: a process which Ngotho, like his son Boro, comes to realise is only possible through violence. Ngugi was gradually becoming critical of the kind of nationalism that was framed in unitary idioms of nationhood and common destiny, but one which deleted any violent struggle from its vocabulary. He was beginning to realise that unless the elite identified with the struggles of the people, unless they abandoned the pursuit of status the way Njoroge does, they ran the risk of being irrelevant. He was also beginning to realise that the elite could not be trusted with the destiny of the nation, and that the kind of heroism that he celebrates in the character of Waiyaki had to be re-examined. This is the point Abdulrazak Gurnah is hinting at when he writes: 'If Boro's bitterness has a histrionic quality, it is because this is part of the ambivalence about the portrayal of the heroic voice' (1993, p.151). Gurnah correctly asserts that '[t]he heroic privileged voice of the visionary in later fiction is handled with suspicion in the earlier novels' (1993, p. 151), and particularly in *A Grain of Wheat* in my view.

In *A Grain of Wheat*, it would appear that Ngugi seeks to redefine heroism and the role of the intellectual political brokers. Although Kihika is one of the most positively portrayed characters in the text, and although his spirit looms larger than the rest of the protagonists, he is certainly not central to the action in the novel. Like Boro in *Weep Not, Child*, Kihika is treated with ambivalence: they are both dismissed as mad (Ngugi 1964, p. 30; Ngugi 1967, pp. 166–7). It is the community of Thabai that is at the centre of *A Grain of Wheat* and every action in the text works to give us some basic insight into this community: its pain and fears of the visible effects of colonialism and possible neocolonialism on the lives of the community; its celebration of the possibility of the birth of a new nation and, indeed, an exploration of the impact of capitalist ideology on the community of Thabai and, by implication, on the Kenyan consciousness. In this text Ngugi locates the political leadership within the vexed relations of the nationalist ideology of the time and the emergent capitalist ideology. Within this context the elite are very much part of a social process whose contradictions and achievements they share with the rest of the community. They are ordinary participants in the community's struggles as opposed to being presented as the sole political brokers whose vision transcends the materiality of the moment and gestures towards a just political dispensation in the future.

One of the reasons why Ngugi makes this shift is because he has come to realise that a liberated Kenya would not escape betrayal and disillusionment embedded in the colonial and neocolonial structures of the country. In one of the captions to the novel Ngugi warns that 'the situation and problems are real – sometimes too painfully real for the peasants who fought the British yet who now see all that they fought for being put on one side'. It was becoming increasingly evident that the complementary roles that the writers and the nationalist politicians enjoyed could not be sustained in the immediate aftermath of independence. As Neil Lazurus reminds us:

It did not take long, after independence, for radical writers to realise that something had gone wrong. They had experienced decolonization as a time of massive transformation. Yet, looking around them in the aftermath they quickly began to perceive that their 'revolution' had been denied ... they came to see that the 'liberation' they had celebrated was cruelly limited in its effects. (1992, p. 18)

This apprehension about Uhuru is best captured in the text by Gikonyo, who during the race that takes place on Uhuru day actually asks himself whether independence is going to make life better for the common man: '"As he ran, Gikonyo tried to hold on to other things ... Would Uhuru bring land into African hands? And would that make a difference to the small man in the village?"' (Ngugi 1967, p. 180). Thus, despite Ngugi's celebration of Uhuru, he cannot hide his displeasure at the imminent betrayal. His apprehension about the decolonisation project is most evident at the scene of Uhuru day celebrations which is marked by gloom and an ominous cloud: 'The morning itself was so dull we feared the day would not break into life' (p. 178).

By casting doubts on Kenya's liberation, Ngugi is moving away from the kind of organic nationalism whose traces we saw in *The River Between*. The attainment of independence, far from leading to an undifferentiated nation-state, threatens to usher in a new form of discrimination that is likely to undermine the interests of the majority of its citizens. The kind of racial identity that informed oppressive political structures in the earlier novels is reversed, if not entirely, in *A Grain of Wheat*. This is not to suggest that Ngugi deletes colonial experience and its debilitating effects from the heart of his most accomplished text. On the contrary, it is his acute awareness of the impact of colonial ideological structures that enables Ngugi to warn against 'the danger at the moment of decolonization ... that despite the departure of the British, colonial and capitalist structures and ideology will continue to shape Kenyans' perceptions. Colonialism will continue under black colonial masters working with white settlers and European powers' (Caminero-Santangelo 1998, p. 144).

Ngugi's insistence that the betrayal which we witness in the body of his text has to be read as a feature inherent in the deep-rooted colonialist structures of oppression and self-interest is significant. It renders all acts of heroism suspect due to a lingering danger of a colonial ideology on the imagination of our would-be heroes of the struggle. What this ideology privileges is individualism and self-interest. It also constructs power around fear and terror as opposed to public accountability. It is Mugo's self-interest and his perceptions of authority as having the capacity to inflict pain that drive him to betray Kihika. Similarly, Gikonyo's alienation from the struggle drives him towards some modest capital accumulation. Gikonyo heralds the emergence of a national bourgeoisie seeking to take advantage of the new money economy and Ngugi's celebration of capital and industry is evident in his admiration of Gikonyo's entrepreneurial qualities:

> At Thabai and villages around Rung'ei, most families finished their harvested food by January. Then there always followed one or two months of drought before the long rains started in March ... that was the time Gikonyo gave up hack-work as a carpenter and entered the market. He went to the market very early in the morning, bought one or two bags of maize at wholesale price from licenced, and at times black-market, maize supplies from the Rift Valley ... With the money obtained, Gikonyo would again haggle for another bag and the two women did the retail selling. (Ngugi 1967, p. 58)

We continue to read that through service and humility, Gikonyo 'coaxed in money' (p. 58). His significance lies in the fact that he is the perfect embodiment of capitalist accu-mulation. He buys, hoards and manipulates his people's needs to his advantage. In the village he becomes the symbol of capitalist ideology: 'The story of Gikonyo's rise to wealth, although on a small scale, carried a moral every mother in Thabai pointed out to her children' (p. 59).

Ngugi seems to make a distinction between Gikonyo's type of accumulation which is played according to basic capitalist rules of demand and supply and that of the MP of Thabai who undercuts his constituents in a deal to buy up the farm of a settler who is leaving for England. The difference also lies in the fact that Gikonyo rallies with other members of the community to form a cooperative, while the MP buys the farm for himself and through unscrupulous means. Gikonyo's cooperative project also gestures towards a more egalitarian form of land ownership which was a popular alternative for land restitution in the 1960s. The system was, however, abused due to the greed of the emergent *petit-bourgeoisie* who, like the MP, were beginning to define themselves by their arrogance and general alienation from the masses on whose behalf they had captured power. This group showed greater loyalty to their foreign masters than to the people who elected them. The MP, for example, fails to join his con-stituents at the Uhuru celebrations because he is entertaining foreign dignitaries in the capital: 'You see, we have so many foreign guests to look after. So apologise to the people for me and say I can't come', the MP tells Gikonyo (Ngugi 1967, p. 63). We also read that '[f]ew MPs had offices in their con-stituencies. As soon as they were elected, they ran to Nairobi and were rarely seen in their areas, except when they came back with other national leaders to address big political rallies' (p. 60). This kind of isolation of the leadership from the masses of the people can only kill the cooperative spirit and the creation of a sense of community that colonialism had fractured.

The significance of Ngugi's text lies precisely in the fact that it seeks to restore the sense of community and to warn against false heroism based on self-interest. To transcend the contradictions embedded in the postcolonial structures of the new nation-state Ngugi posits a process of introspection and the forging of a communal consciousness based on honesty and integrity. These are the qualities that virtually all characters in the text lack. To avoid the reproduction of degraded values and abuse of trust epitomised in the character of the MP, the people of Thabai must be reconnected to themselves. And here Ngugi is not talking about an organic return to the source, but a realistic acceptance of multiple histories that the people of Thabai share as a precondition for its regeneration. Gikonyo and Mumbi, the erstwhile founders of the Agikuyu community, lead this process of healing through the sharing of their personal histories. It is Mumbi's confession in particular that eventually inspires Mugo to lay his soul bare to the couple and later to the community of Thabai. We are told that '[s]he had sat there, and talked to him and given him a glimpse of a new earth. She had trusted him, and confided in him. This simple trust had forced him to tell her the truth' (Ngugi 1967, p. 234). The 'new earth' has a double meaning in this context. The new Kenyan state seems to be poised between a society that seeks to perpetuate the values of the old colonial order and that which seeks to reconstitute itself by enforcing the virtues of communal responsibility. If the nationalist elite have betrayed the emergent Kenyan nation through selfishness and corruption, then the rest of the community must cling to the vision of a 'new earth' that inspired the liberation struggle in the first place. That is why the last section of the novel entitled 'Harambee' – pulling together – is ironic. Ironic because the Kenyan leaders who created the slogan at the moment of liberation have failed to live up to its meaning. And yet Ngugi insists that the communal spirit celebrated in the slogan remains relevant. The section represents the possibility of rebirth because it dramatises the healing process that Gikonyo has initiated with his estranged wife, Mumbi. To do this Gikonyo must shed the values of self-interest and begin to pull along with Mumbi in the restoration of the Agikuyu community and the broader Kenyan nation that it symbolises. It is these communal values, humane and people-oriented, that become the centre-piece of Ngugi's later novels.

However, in Ngugi's later texts, whose rhetorics would seem to privilege the voice of the people – the marginalised workers and peasants – the role of the elite changes. As opposed to being the voice of the nationalist project, the elite continue to be the mediating figure between the class aspirations of the oppressed and the exploitative ideology of the neocolonial *petit-bourgeois* class. In other words, if alienation and self-interest of the elite undermined the agency of the ruling elite, if they made heroism suspect, Ngugi seems to be suggesting that a new form of heroism, which would put the interests of the people at the centre of his narratives, is required. And, indeed, the socialist alternative to capitalism would seem to have offered Ngugi the intellectual return to the importance of the elite, except this time round Ngugi draws a distinction between the progressive elite – the revolutionary ideologue of the people – and the retrogressive elite, which has joined hands with the former colonial masters to exploit the people. Ngugi seems to imply that the elite cannot be constituted as an undifferentiated group. And yet Ngugi's return to heroism that he deflates in *A Grain of Wheat* is not without its contradictions, as I will attempt to show in the section that follows. The celebration of the communal spirit that is central to the critique of the colonial and neocolonial presence in *A Grain of Wheat* is undermined by his return to a Waiyaki-type of ideologue and the deleting of the community from the centre-stage of his narrative.

The Return of Heroism and the Crisis of the African Revolution

> So it is that after the poisoned gift of independence, radical African writers like Ousmane, or like Ngugi in Kenya, find themselves back in the dilemma of ... bearing a passion for change and social regeneration which has not yet found its agents. I hope it is clear that this is also very much an aesthetic dilemma, a crisis of representation: it was not difficult to identify an adversary who spoke another language and wore the visible trappings of colonial occupation. (Jameson 1991, p. 98)

When in 1981 Ngugi lamented the absence of positive heroes in African literature, heroes who would 'embody the spirit of struggle and resistance against exploitation' (1981b, p. 24), I believe he was admitting, albeit unwittingly and unconsciously, that there was no strong tradition of the working class in Africa and, indeed, no revolutionary leadership that would lead Africa out of its political and economic crises. The absence of positive heroes in African literature, I would argue, was ample evidence of a basic lack: not necessarily of heroes that would embody the spirit of struggle and resistance as such, but rather a good indication of the absence of the working-class heroes that would champion the type of socialist transformation that Ngugi had in mind when he made the lament.[1] It was an expression of a desire to bring about the kind of radical change, 'the upward thrust of the people' (Lazarus 1992, p.15), that Fanon had anticipated, moving historically toward self-determination and bringing into completion the African revolution that independence had failed to deliver. But as Neil Lazarus argues, 'the historical fact that the 'upward thrust of the people' was not maintained in the post-colonial era, points to the conclusion that it was never really present as a revolutionary force in the first place' (p. 15).

And herein lies the dilemma of a radical writer in Africa that Jameson draws our attention to. This was a dilemma because this group of radical African intellectuals, having cast themselves as revolutionaries, 'became convinced', writes Lazarus, 'that they, not the rest of their class, had history on their side. This imbued them with a new sense of purpose, since they saw themselves as representing the voice of the revolution' (1991, p. 11). But as Jameson correctly points out, it was not enough simply to have a passion for change and regeneration in a postcolonial space which had not nurtured agents for social change or for the radical social transformation that writers like Ngugi had hoped for.[2]

It seems to me that nothing illustrates Ngugi's dilemma and uncertainties better than his portrayal of the so-called forces of regeneration or agents of transformation. One of the major rifts in Ngugi's postcolonial narrative is the romantic portrayal of the working-class leaders and his inability to give workers and peasants a concrete representation in his narrative. In his postcolonial novels, Ngugi demonstrates that there is resistance by workers and peasants against their oppression which creates the conditions for an imminent revolution. The revolutionary possibilities are embodied in the workers led by Karega in *Petals of Blood*, Muturi in *Devil on the Cross* and Matigari in *Matigari*.

I intend to examine the portrayal of Ngugi's heroes and the oppressed workers and peasants against the background of fragmentation. I will attempt to show that his portrayal of the working-class heroes and the workers that they lead is both romantic and abstract. I will further show that Ngugi's creative dilemma manifests itself in a crisis of aesthetic representation of heroes in which Ngugi's typical hero is invested with positive qualities, presented as faultless, selfless and courageous. The heroes are highly schematic and stereotyped: they are always the embodiment of a tradition of struggle and sacrifice. Ngugi's crisis also tends to manifest itself in the abstract construction of workers and their struggle. Ngugi's workers experience monopoly capitalism and imperialism, not concrete lived experiences. This portrayal, I will argue, reduces them to abstract concepts rather than 'specific individuals and groups' with 'specific conflicts and struggles' (Scott 1985, p. 43). The chapter will attempt to give a brief comparison between Ngugi and Sembene Ousmane. I will, for example, argue that in Sembene's *God's Bits of Wood*, the workers feel the direct impact of the machines on their lives and they have concrete grievances. The actual transformation of workers in Sembene's text takes place within the context of their struggle, a struggle in which various groups across gender, class and age come to terms with the weight of the historic moment and how they are implicated in it.

Ngugi's Heroes: The Example of Karega in Petals of Blood

One of the major defining features of Ngugi's narrative, particularly in the later novels, is its highly schematic and predictable portrayal of heroes and heroines. They are, like most of Ngugi's characters, socially determined character types which follow a special scheme within the narrative. They often come from a family and social background of deprivation, poverty and endless suffering which they are always battling to change for the common good of humanity. To this extent, their lives are also marked by rebellion and resistance to domination. We have Matigari in *Matigari*, Muturi in *Devil on the Cross* and Karega in *Petals of Blood*.

Karega, in *Petals of Blood*, is a good example. His name translated means 'the one who refused' or 'the rebel'. As a youth he took part in the strike against Mr Fraudsham at Siriana High School and he also masterminded the strike against Chui, the first black headmaster of Siriana. Munira describes him as a young man full of idealism, hope and vitality – a man with a 'glowing faith in the possibilities of heroism and devotion' (Ngugi 1977, p. 46). Karega's idealism and search for truth and justice dominate the text. This search, we read, 'made him a wanderer all over Kenya, from Mombasa to Kisumu and back again to Ilmorog' (p. 46). There is a definite interplay between quest and rebellion in Karega's character.

The interplay between quest and rebellion is best played out when Karega takes up his teaching post in Munira's school and he seeks to transform the school syllabus, almost on his own and without the involvement of Munira. Karega sees his first duty at school as that of raising the consciousness of the children by teaching them the history of Ilmorog and showing them its interconnectedness to the broader Kenyan society, and to Africa in general. He soon comes to the realisation that his lessons are abstract, given the disquieting silence of the pupils. He discovers that his approach to teaching raises more questions than answers and opens up numerous silences and rifts within his own educational heritage from Siriana. Karega is eager to evolve a syllabus that has a strong bias toward the 'African continent' without being conscious of the limitations and strengths of such a syllabus. When the lawyer sends him history books by black intellectuals, he discovers that it is not enough to be black in order to write objectively on the history of the blacks. The production of knowledge, Karega discovers, is not neutral, but serves specific interests and groups. As the lawyer tells him: 'In a situation of the robber and the robbed, in a situation in which the old man of the sea is sitting on Sinbad, there can be no neutral history and politics. If you would learn look about you: choose your side' (Ngugi 1977, p. 200). By playing on Karega's quest for truth, Ngugi takes us through a predictable path of knowledge for those of us who are familiar with Ngugi's discourses on Kenyan history. Karega is gradually forced to come to terms with history as a contested terrain between the robber and the robbed (see Ngugi 1981b, pp. 123–9). Predictably, Karega's ideological outlook begins to change when Munira dismisses him unceremoniously from his teaching post at Ilmorog Primary School and he decides that he has a contribution to make towards the struggle of workers to come.

It is, however, after his struggles as a worker all over Kenya, we read, that Karega is radically transformed. When he returns to Ilmorog after five years of self-imposed exile he starts a trade union as a vehicle for raising the awareness of workers in Theng'eta Breweries where he works as an accounting clerk. The formation of a trade union which leads to the worker's strike, which we encounter at the beginning of the novel, would seem to be a culmination in a linear process in Karega's character development, a development directed by the twin semes of quest and rebellion which cut across his life again and again.

And yet Karega's coming to consciousness, his apparent transformation from a black nationalist to a trade union leader embracing the socialist vision, remains unconvincing. This is largely because as a character most associated with the mass movement, indeed as a character who, in the words of Gikandi, 'mediates between the inner reality of the novel and the author's ontology' (1987, p. 138), his impact on the narrative as the centre of consciousness remains contrived and abstract. For one, much of what we are told about Karega is filtered through the character of Munira whom the writer discredits as weak in mind, jealous and unreliable. In fact, the narrative voice, the omniscient narrator, is constantly and deliberately pushing us to see things from Karega's perspective because the other protagonists cannot be trusted. Karega is revealed through the rhetoric of the narrative which asserts his heroism now and again, and through his unmediated polemical speeches which set him apart from the rest, as a man with a mission. When, for example, Munira calls Wanja a prostitute, Karega is enraged and rebukes him in a speech that Munira correctly describes as 'sermons and moral platitudes' (Ngugi 1977, p. 240).

The moral sermonising goes on and on and, in the end, the narrative voice concurs and we are told: 'There followed another moment of silence embarrassing to Munira because once again he felt on trial, that he had been placed on a moral balance and had been found wanting' (Ngugi 1977, p. 241). Within this deliberate scheme, the authorial voice under the guise of the narrator systematically undermines the moral stature of the other protagonists close to Karega, while at the same time underscoring Karega's moral superiority. Karega becomes a tool for political mediation in the narrative in the hands of the writer, and yet what Karega says reads like abstract philosophical reflections on an individual's turbulent consciousness. We do not seem to come to grips fully with what shapes this consciousness. This is further compounded by the fact that much of what happens in the life of Karega is neither dramatised nor given adequate representation in the narrative. His journeys across the length and breadth of Kenya are reported in very general terms and yet they form the basis of Karega's social transformation. For the best part of the narrative Karega is not centre-stage and yet his consciousness rules the narrative. I think the basic weaknesses with Karega's portrayal, which set him apart as a highly romanticised figure, are the writer's failure to anchor Karega's struggle in Ilmorog where the text is set and also the failure to give a concrete representation to the peasants and workers whose lives Karega seeks to influence. In many ways, he is larger than life and isolated or simply overshadows the experiences of those people that he ought to be leading.

When an author chooses a particular setting for his or her novel, it shows they believe that the physical setting of the narrative has an important function to play in the novel. I believe Ngugi chose the village of Ilmorog as the centre-stage to re-enact Kenya's history and to show how imperialist domination has ravaged colonial and postcolonial Kenya. Ilmorog is therefore a microcosm of Kenya; it is supposed to represent the larger Kenyan setting. Within the context of the African narrative where the rural peasants are often marginalised or simply ignored, Ngugi's choice of a rural village signals an attempt to place Kenyan peasants at the centre of his narratives. And indeed, as a physical entity,

Ilmorog village looms large in the narrative, as something close to a living character, with its moments of misery and joy, with its epochs of sterility and fertility which have profoundly affected the lives of its inhabitants. As the narrative has it, the peasants of Ilmorog always made history by 'taming' nature's resources, fighting the vagaries of nature and celebrating their moments of joy and triumph through dance and song, in praise of their 'founders' (Ngugi 1977, p. 120).

The graphic picture of the old and new Ilmorog, with its glorious past and degraded present, is not fully utilised in character development or even in depicting the dynamics of social struggle within Ilmorog as the centre-stage. I do not concur with Gikandi's conclusion, in an otherwise illuminating piece on 'Character and consciousness in *Petals of Blood*', that 'Karega's relationship with Ilmorog is active', because 'he relates to the town and its people in such a way that they shape his vision and understanding of the neo-colonial situation' (Gikandi 1987, p. 138). Surely Karega's first fundamental change comes as a result of a letter written to him by the lawyer, an outsider to Ilmorog, whom Gikandi has correctly described as an 'authorial puppet ... a thinly disguised instrument of authorial consciousness whose failure as a fictional persona has serious implications on character and consciousness in the political novel' (p. 140). The second and most profound change in Karega's character takes place outside the narrative after a five-year period of self-exile from Ilmorog. Where is the active relationship between Karega and the people of Ilmorog, one may venture to ask? And who are the people of Ilmorog?

Throughout the novel, except for Nyakinyua, the people of Ilmorog are merely on the periphery as onlookers. Karega is presented as the silent primary mover, breaking the barriers of ethnic enclaves and of subservience to capital which have prevented the workers from uniting for their rights all along. And in all these, not a single worker is mentioned and yet the impact of Karega's crusade was so great that Karega himself was elected as the Secretary General of the Union, and 'the victory of the Breweries Workers' Union had a very traumatic effect on the hitherto docile workers of Ilmorog' (Ngugi 1977, p. 305).

Like the workers and peasants of Ilmorog, the employers are equally invisible. The only time we have a superficial encounter with the directors of Theng'eta Breweries is when they are locked in a perverse sexual struggle over Wanja in which they are manipulated to their death. Thus the struggle in Ilmorog, which should be a communal experience and a dramatisation of the conflict between labour and capital, remains an abstract experience in which the relationship between the communal ideologue, Karega, the workers and the rest of the marginalised groups is not given adequate expression. The failure to give concrete expression to social conflict and the building of worker consciousness intimated in the text undermines the dialectical interplay between the forces at work.

In contrast, in Ousmane's *God's Bits of Wood* we see workers, who hitherto had been very passive, becoming active and organising themselves to confront the owners of the machine which had for so long dominated their lives. Their ability to organise themselves and engage in an active struggle, thereby bringing to a halt the machine, transforms them. In the process of the strike they regain their human worth when at last they discover their strength in the collective endeavour and their dialectical dependence on the machine. In talking about the social transformation of the workers, the narrative voice tells us that 'they began to understand that the machine was making of them a whole new breed of men. It did not belong to them; it was they who belonged to it' (Ousmane 1970, p. 52).

The significance of Sembene Ousmane's text lies in the fact that although it attempts to negotiate the relationship between trade union recognition and anticolonial agitation; between class consciousness and the organisation of a nation; it is steeped in the concrete experience of workers. As Craig Smith (1993, pp. 51–6) writes, Ousmane is able to explore 'the impact of technology on African life' as a force that not 'only alienates the workers from their traditional labour, ... [but] shapes them into modern individuals who can participate in the modern discourse of technology' (in this case the railway) that the French capital had always denied them. At the same time, the machine enables them to become aware of themselves as a new class with a new measure of agency in the larger discourse of money economy which now organises their lives. I believe the quality of Ousmane's text rests on the fact that he recreates a railway workers' strike which occurred between October 1947 and March 1948 on the Dakar–Niger railway line and in the process he examines how various institutions, classes, people and individuals are affected by this singular experience. It is also Ousmane's ability to render visible the basic lives of his characters, their experiences and contradictions, without losing sight of the collective strike through which the concrete experiences are unveiled, that endears us to the significance of the historic moment of the narrative.

It seems to me that Ngugi's central characters, particularly Karega, are linked to the setting and the central subjects of the narrative – the workers and peasants of Ilmorog – by a very weak cord. There seems to be a contradiction between the collective and the individual character experiences since the individual experiences appear to overshadow the collective experience. And yet, the narrative clearly points to the fact that Ngugi is seeking to dramatise and to mediate the collective struggle of the people of Ilmorog. The story of *Petals of Blood* is therefore the story of Ilmorog, its growth and development. Yet the peasants of Ilmorog are not at the centre of the story. Neither are the workers at the centre of the new Ilmorog. And although the writer is constantly evoking the collective through the 'we' narrative voice, it is nothing less than a ploy for authorial intrusion; a strategy for asserting the ideological authority of the writer in the narrative. Even Gikandi – a critic sympathetic to Ngugi's characterisation – concedes that the authorial 'intrusiveness is even apparent in some of the characters' thoughts and words' and that occasionally 'the novelist misuses his omniscient authority, becomes unequivocal and forces situations and characters to fit into a predetermined ideological position' (Gikandi 1987, p. 146). A good example of a crude ideological imposition on a character's consciousness is to be found in the last scene of the narrative focusing on Karega's reflections in the cell. In this passage, in which 'Imperialism' and 'capitalism' are slated in the most grotesque terms as systems 'that bred hordes of round-bellied jiggers and bedbugs with parasitism and cannibalism' (Ngugi 1977, p. 344), Ngugi's voice is undisguised. Coming as it does at the end of the narrative, the passage also gives Ngugi the last chance to reiterate the ideological perspective that he has been trying to push through the character of Karega. The veiled voice of the omniscient narrator replaces that of the character and gives the writer the liberty to jar our imagination as readers with authorial ideology under the guise of a character's conscious-ness. Again, the reference to workers and peasants is deprived of any concrete expression because they are conspicuously absent in the narrative. Akinyi, the woman worker who appears briefly at the beginning and at the end of the narrative with a message of solidarity, is a poor attempt to cover up for the workers' absence. She stands for the undramatised heroism of the workers that the narrative voice intimates.

Karega's portrayal isolates him as a romantic figure who shoulders the burden of the community and works towards its transformative hour of redemption. In this transformative process championed by the selected few, the marginalised groups are not part of the central discourse. This brings me to the second major issue in this chapter: a critical assessment of Ngugi's portrayal of the workers and the oppressed in general.

Imagining the Subaltern Under Conditions of Marginality and Displacement

No one doubts Ngugi's commitment to a complete overhaul of the postcolonial state. The author's dilemma lies precisely in the fact that Kenyan society does not afford him a tradition of a working-class struggle or a literary tradition directed primarily at bringing about socialist transformation. Instead, we have workers' and peasants' struggles in Kenya scattered across its historical landscape. These struggles were by no means representing uniform goals and interests, and certainly not a socialist transformation in such absolute terms as Ngugi tends to suggest. Ngugi's predicament lies in the impracticality of trying to forge a coherent vision for change in the face of fragmentation, displacement and a basic absence of models to inspire his writing. This leads Ngugi in two directions which have become predictable in his narrative. First, Ngugi projects unity and a coordinated political will onto the masses by creating in them a voluntary awareness of their plight, and he endows them with a revolutionary consciousness that is not fully anchored in their material reality, even as they work towards a revolution that is imminent. Second, the workers are conceptualised in abstract terms.

In both *Petals of Blood* and *Devil on the Cross* the workers and the management are faceless. We do not have a visible representation of workers other than the mass of people chanting anti-imperialist slogans. The management is known simply as imperialist exploiters and the workers as the producers. If the slogans of enraged workers at the beginning of *Petals of Blood* are anything to go by, then we ought to know these workers better. We need to live with them through their experience beyond the slogans and feel with them the brutality of the management that has brought about the tragic encounter at the start of the narrative.

Ngugi's workers do not seem to go through tangible experiences which affect their lives directly. They experience capitalism and imperialism, two concepts that they do not appear to be fully capable of conceptualising. The strike in *Petals of Blood* which takes place at the brewery seems to be directed at a faceless management. The workers' coming to awareness is also the sole work of an individual character, Karega, in spite of his silence and withdrawal. In *Devil on the Cross* we have Muturi, the one character who promises to approximate the ideal portrait of a worker, at least from his background and experiences with Wariinga, but the writer abandons the more personal and individualised line of characterisation of Muturi and falls for abstract representation. Like most of Ngugi's revolutionary heroes Muturi remains extremely one-dimensional. He has a good disposition and is kind by nature. He rescues Wariinga from two suicide attempts, and helps the old woman, Wangari, with the fare for the *matatu* taxi. When we encounter him in the text, he displays the confidence and insight of a seasoned activist.

And yet, all we know about him is that he has travelled widely all over Kenya and that he is a carpenter. And although Muturi is said to belong to a secret workers' organisation, we hardly feel the presence of these workers, even in their underground world. The only glimpse we get of them is when they join the students' demonstration against the thieves in the cave. The 'great organization of the workers and peasants' (Ngugi 1982, p. 204) that we read of is hardly dramatised.

The portrayal of Ngugi's worker-leaders like Muturi leaves one with very little room for critical insight into the situation of their lot. Muturi's position is predictable – employers are parasites and workers are producers; employers are the devil and workers are the angels who must drive the devil out of this earth. The workers produce guns, only to be used by the capitalist exploiters to kill workers (Ngugi 1982, p. 211). This moral position is repeated over and over again. Njabulo Ndebele describes this type of representation as being underpinned by 'moral ideology' which, he rightly observes, 'tends to ossify complex social problems into symbols which are perceived as finished forms of good or evil, instead of leading us towards important necessary insights into the social processes leading to those finished forms' (1991, p. 23).

The weakness of Ngugi's characterisation scheme in which oppressors are portrayed as evil and workers as good is that it tends to obscure certain contradictions among the workers themselves. One tendency is to portray workers as absolutely humane and generous in spirit, as in the case of Muturi. The other tendency is to take the workers' consciousness as a given, with the end result that their struggle is often romanticised. The romantic portrayal of workers becomes obvious, precisely because of their conspicuous absence at the centre-stage of Ngugi's narratives. The vacuum is often filled by the positive heroes who are larger than life and apparently embody the spirit of struggle, but of a struggle which finds little backing from workers within the narrative. In striking contrast, Ousmane's depiction of the collective struggle in *God's Bits of Wood* is far from romantic. The striking workers have their own contradictions which threaten the spirit of the strike. There are those who put their personal interests first and threaten the strike. Diara is the first casualty. He takes his share of the money from the strike committee but goes back to work. Beaugosse, who for quite some time is an official of the workers' union and a respected leader of the delegates from Dakar at the union's first meeting with the railway officials, abandons the struggle and takes sides with the oppressors. Sounkare, the oldest worker in the company, cannot join the strike for legitimately human reasons and his profound human tragedy touches us the more when he dies like a neglected dog. Even leaders like Doudou and Tiemoko are for some time driven by their personal egos more than the general good of the society, although they learn to subordinate their selfish drives to the greater struggle of the community. Indeed, even the much revered worker-leader, Bakayoko, by participating in this heroic struggle, transforms his family relations and begins to rethink the trappings of patriarchy in the form of polygamy. Unlike Ngugi, Ousmane's depiction of the striking workers draws attention to the subtle experiences that inform their lives beyond the theoretical jargon. He is able to show how people change through struggle, and also to draw attention to the fact that people respond to the concrete realities of their situation rather than some abstract phenomenon. What is celebrated is the workers' self-taught radicalism, born out of their suffering and awakening of the workers themselves. In the words of Piven and Cloward, workers like all human beings:

> experience deprivation and oppression within a concrete setting, not as the end product of large and abstract processes, and it is the concrete experience that moulds their discontent into specific grievances against specific targets. Workers experience the factory, the speeding rhythm of the assembly line, the foremen, the spies, the guards, the owner, and the pay cheque. They do not experience monopoly capitalism. (cited in Scott 1985, p. 43)

Piven's and Cloward's point is at the heart of Ngugi's dilemma because Ngugi denies his workers the kind of concrete portrayal that would situate their lives and experiences within a specific context of work, of daily routine and of conflict and struggle. It is within a concrete setting that we come to terms with the forms of resistance that mark people's lives. It is at the level of practical experience, rather than the philosophical level, that class struggle is waged. Again, Ousmane's portrayal of the railway workers and their strike is relevant here. The workers strike because of specific grievances: better wages, pensions and allowances for their families. They identify the French management of the railway line as their immediate enemy. Significantly again, both 'worker and manager share and contest one discursive space' (Smith 1993, p. 55) as reflected in the physical proximity of the worker and manager, thereby heightening the awareness of difference. In this confrontation, 'they have to acknowledge one another in the same discursive space' (p. 55). He shows how the nature of French colonialism manifests itself best in the specific confrontation between the railway management and workers. In the process Ousmane restores agency back to the colonised subject through the workers' struggle around which the whole society is mobilised to fight injustice and colonial oppression.

In *Petals of Blood*, the journey to Nairobi, organised by the Ilmorog community when they are afflicted by drought, also comes close to the idea of a social struggle located within a practical experience to which I am referring. The march is one of those very few compelling moments in the narrative in which the people of Ilmorog demonstrate their discontent with authority. The people are mobilised around a concrete problem. And when they arrive in Nairobi, they go to their local MP, and not the government or some imaginary enemy. Significantly, it is a march about a phenomenon that is currently affecting their lives in a very direct way; it is a march for survival of the people, of their animals and an expression of the value they attach to the now scorched land of their ancestors. It is therefore proper that the elders should see this march as a continuation of their historical struggle. More than any other event in the narrative, this journey affects the lives of the characters and the whole community of Ilmorog. Except for Nyakinyua, it is the only time that we meet the other peasants like Muriuki, Njuguna, Ruoro, Njogu and Muturi. Similar experiences that depict the direct involvement of the people are hard to come by in the text.

To encapsulate, Ngugi's *Petals of Blood* resembles Sembene Ousmane's *God's Bits of Wood* both in its ideological concerns and, to a large extent, in its subject. But in contrast to Ngugi's, in Ousmane's novel there is a relationship between a specific sociohistorical subject and the individual character experiences, to the extent that the individual experiences and consciousness are shaped by the ongoing social struggle.[3] Even the sense of alienation displayed by certain characters is related directly to the central and political action of the novel. Neither in *Petals of Blood* nor in *Devil on the Cross* do we come across workers or even peasants who are directly linked to the political action of the novel.

There are two possible reasons for Ngugi's inability to dramatise the working-class struggle. One is that Kenya has not developed a class-conscious and organised working class and so Ngugi has nothing to fall back on. In the absence of an organised working class he creates his ideal working class to fill the gap and in the process deals with it at an abstract level. The second is that Ngugi, as a political activist, desires and wills a revolution that would lead to a total overthrow of the capitalist system in Kenya and he therefore uses the narrative form to negotiate the possible revolutionary strategies that he would wish to see used by the oppressed in Kenya. In doing so, he is forced to create an imaginary revolutionary working class modelled after the socialist revolutions.

Although the two factors may both have something to do with Ngugi's aesthetic dilemma, I find the first point more compelling than the latter because it concerns the legacy of colonialism and, by extension, the crisis of the postcolonial state in Africa. Indeed, the dominant text in much of the postcolonial narrative in Africa would seem to trace the present social and economic crisis in Africa to the conditions of displacement and fragmentation that were engendered by colonialism on the continent. At the heart of the crisis is the stark reality that colonialism left backward economies that could hardly nurture an advanced proletariat. The nascent working class still had roots in the peasantry: it was a class that never saw itself as a social group with a historical mission to bring about the kind of fundamental social transformation that Ngugi tends to thrust upon them in his narrative. The burden of ensuring historical transformation had never been taken seriously and consciously by the working classes in Africa, precisely because the colonial economy and its structures, which were inherited almost intact at independence, never encouraged or prepared them for such a mission. The new political leadership – the African elite created out of the colonial womb – was equally ill-prepared for political governance. It was a class of bastards which had no identity of its own, but had to take up leadership at independence, torn as it were between its desire for continuity and the interests of the masses on whose behalf it had claimed power. Born out of the ruins of colonial history, the postcolonial state was a society whose agents of change lacked a coherent vision, whether from the point of view of the working class or from the ruling elite that were shepherded into power at independence.

Conclusion

Ngugi's response has been to give form to this state of 'chaos' by attempting to reconstitute history out of fragmentation; to reconstruct this history out of the colonial ruins. And yet the dilemma of the radical writer in Africa, the writer of praxis that Fredrick Jameson so aptly alludes to in his controversial article on Third World literature, is evident in Ngugi's writing. Ngugi, like many African writers, is groping for a vision that would give expression to the state of displacement and fragmentation on the continent. The predicament of radical writers is compounded by the fact that they have no models of radical transformation or class war in the postcolonial state to inspire them. The crisis of African nationalism and the failure of the African revolution that Fanon has written so much about is a pointer to the continuing state of fragmentation in Africa (Fanon 1967, pp. 116–65).

The problematic of Ngugi's revolutionary theory – his strategies for transformation – has to be located in the difficult task of trying to create sense out of the state of fragmentation. This process of trying to piece together history out of broken fragments, as I have pointed out following Walter Benjamin, always leads to an allegorical return to the past.

Ngugi's constant return to the past – to the Mau Mau war – could be linked to his attempt to reconstitute the ideal agents of change. Indeed, his superficial portrayal of the peasantry and workers, and his tendency to project a unity and coordinated political will upon them from above, could also be traced to the state of fragmentation and the writer's inability to forge a coherent transformative vision in the face of social displacement.

Conclusion

History is Subversive

> ... it is precisely because history is the result of struggle and
> tells of change that it is perceived as a threat by all the
> ruling strata in all the oppressive exploitative systems.
> Tyrants and the tyrannical systems are terrified at the
> sound of the wheels of history. History is subversive. And
> it is because it is actually subversive of the existing
> tyrannical system that there have been attempts to arrest it.
> (Ngugi 1993, pp. 96–7)

Ngugi's belief in the supremacy of historical change and the
use of narrative as a tool for ordering and shaping history is
evident in all the texts studied in this book. Ngugi believes
that the narrative provides a space within which an historical
meaning can be contested. And because narrative provides
space for contesting meaning, it is an important tool for
teaching and mobilising people; a tool for drawing people's
attention to social meaning, their role and function in the
process of shaping and making history. By implicating people
– and by 'people' I mean the marginalised classes of Africa
denied historical agency by imperialism and its agents in
Africa – Ngugi is challenging the linear historiography that
has tended to repress the voice of the ruled while privileging
the debilitating narratives of colonial conquest in Africa. He
does this in two significant ways: one, by insisting and
showing that the fundamental substance of history is change
and, two, by positing historical movement as a threat to
absolute power. In both senses, Ngugi challenges those
historical readings which seek to freeze history and to turn it
into official dogma for control and submission. This is what
Ngugi means when he asserts that 'history is subversive'

(Ngugi 1993, p. 97) because it undermines relations of domination by restoring agency to the ruled and exposing the rulers for what they really are. At the heart of Ngugi's narrative, as I have argued, is an assertion of his people's history beyond the simplistic cultural contestation that we tend to associate with literary artefacts.

In his earlier texts, I have shown that Ngugi is keenly concerned with how colonial categories of knowledge flattened the complex experiences of the African people and he therefore sets out to put the record straight. Attempts at recovering African gnosis by evoking the Agikuyu mythology, while striving for a new mythos rooted in contemporary experience engendered by colonialism, is at the heart of Ngugi's earlier novels. For Ngugi, the reconstruction of African knowledge involves, as Edward Said puts it, 'the rediscovery and repatriation of what had been suppressed in the natives' past by the processes of imperialism' (1994, p. 253), as well as the appropriation of those intellectual protocols and the social institutions that came with colonialism. Thus, when Ngugi agonises over the idea of a nation-state called Kenya, he is agonising over a geographic space 'designed and redesigned by explorers from Europe for generations' (p. 253). This, Edward Said reminds us, 'is the partial tragedy of resistance, that it must to a certain degree work to recover forms already established or at least influenced or infiltrated by the culture of the empire' (p. 253). Ngugi's earlier narratives, I have argued, involved a process of reimagining a new geographic and political space. His writings were contingent upon the social and political exigencies of the time which demanded the urgent invention of national identities. This process was multifaceted and complex because it involved not only the act of reconstituting Africa from the ruins of colonial plunder, but also a critical engagement with those discursive practices and political structures that came with colonialism. This process of social engineering, I have argued, was both backward- and forward-looking because it was neither a total rejection of tradition nor an outright condemnation of those aspects of colonialism that had given the necessary impetus to the modernist projects. The uneasy relationship between inward-looking nationalism and the modernist project rooted in colonialist ideologies and structures that I have explored in Ngugi's earlier novels has a lot to do with the complexity of the issues that confronted African writers in the decade before and during the immediate aftermath of independence. And whatever one might think of Ngugi's earlier texts, it is clear that in these texts the Kenyan writer positions himself as part of that process of history-making in Africa. His attempts to reconcile ethnic and national identities, individualist and communal interests, were all part of that imaginative process to redefine the historic destiny of the continent and find one's place within it.

In the process of this search for historical relevance and the remapping of Africa's historical contours, Ngugi, in his later texts, revises the metanarrative of nationalist ideology of the period before and after independence. In its place, Ngugi reconstitutes the nationalist struggle as the heroic narrative of workers and peasants. The theme of 'resistance' to imperialism remains the basic plot element, but he rewrites it, particularly in his later novels, as the concerted struggle of the colonised subjects operating on the margins of power. Ngugi is doing what his 'progressive' counterparts in history have called 'history from below', that is, the restoration of voice to the ruled classes in Africa, voices that had been submerged in the colonialist reconfiguration of the continent and the meta-narratives of the nationalism. The allegorical resurrection of the Kimathi figure in virtually all his novels and the mythical return of Matigari – the Mau Mau remnant that survived – in his more recent novel of the same title, underpins this narrative of sacrifice and redemption by the oppressed of Africa. And on this Ngugi is unequivocal: 'If there is one consistent theme in the history of Kenya over the last four hundred years or so (since the sixteenth century), it is surely one of the Kenyan people's struggle against foreign domination' (Ngugi 1993, p. 97). This theme is, Ngugi avers, 'the *real living* history of the masses' as opposed to 'the *approved official* history' (p. 98). The theme is unambiguously African resistance to imperialism.

It is no accident, therefore, that Ngugi should, in his later novels, place great emphasis on resistance as the major plot element in a continuous narrative of African history. Specifically, as I have shown, he argues for a connection between 'primary resistance movements' in the early days of colonisation and 'modern mass nationalism' that followed in the later days of colonialism. The linear connection, as I have attempted to show, is captured best in Ngugi's constant display of anticolonial war heroes from Africa and the black diaspora, ranging from Chaka, Toussaint, Nat Turner, Laibon Turugat, to Nkrumah and Cabral (Ngugi 1977, p. 137). The grand narrative of African resistance, the great refusal as Frederick Cooper is wont to call it, is crystallised in the Mau Mau war in Kenya. For Ngugi, it is the Mau Mau resistance movement that broke the back of British colonialism because, as an armed struggle to reclaim land appropriated by the British, it was a radical rejection of British occupation in Kenya. And yet, as I have argued, Kenyan historiography has turned around the debate and attempted to draw attention, instead, on how various meanings of Mau Mau have been shaped in the production of knowledge in colonial and post-colonial Kenya. And whether one agrees with those debates which challenge and support the interpretation of Mau Mau as a truly nationalist movement is beside the point. For Ngugi, the Mau Mau war provides a template upon which the disparate segments of Kenyan history are brought to order. Mau Mau was the beginning of a moral and material struggle for self-definition by all those oppressed by tyrants throughout the continent.

What Ngugi has done is to turn Mau Mau into an icon, a central symbol around which the allegorisation of Kenyan history is built and given shape. If British colonists turned the Mau Mau war into a figure of degeneration and a reversal to atavism, Ngugi turns the debate on its head and appropriates the Mau Mau war in his subversion of colonial and neocolonial power structures in modern Kenya. Through his allegorisation of Kenyan history, the present struggle against neocolonial structures reconfigures earlier movements for social justice and gestures towards a future Kenya free from the oppression. This, in turn, has meant that Ngugi adopts a linear historical perspective which is in part determined by a linear typology which allegory generally imposes to constrain the reader's ability to construct meaning beyond that which is given. I have argued that Ngugi's recourse to allegory could be traced to the state of fragmentation engendered by the crisis of the so-called African revolution and the political paralysis after independence and, indeed, to the fact that Ngugi, as a writer of praxis and political activist, has suffered at the hands of two successive regimes in Kenya. He was detained and he has spent close to two decades in exile. And yet, these notwithstanding, Ngugi's project of historical subversion, I argue, runs the risk of flattening the lives of the colonised subjects in Africa due to this linearity of vision.

What emerges in my analysis of Ngugi's later novels is a broad binary opposition between forces of oppression on the one hand and forces of resistance on the other. The complexity of social relations that we find in *A Grain of Wheat*, for example, is abandoned in the later novels and instead of capturing the ambivalent relationship between the colonial state and the so-called collaborators on the one hand, and the ambivalent relationship between the comprador bourgeoisie, the postcolonial state and the forces of global imperialism on the other, Ngugi succumbs to linear presentation of the collaboration/resistance dyad which deletes any possibilities of subversion and deflection of power within those structures established by colonialism. I have also argued in the same vein that Ngugi's understanding of class conflict in Kenya is too deeply embedded in dependency theory to allow for a nuanced understanding of the complex colonial and postcolonial experience in Kenya.

It is difficult to believe that response to colonialism did not rise beyond the collective or grand resistance to imperialism. And yet one of the impressions created in Ngugi's more recent narratives is that Africans did not have any lives outside the parameters set by colonial power structures; that Africans were virtually reduced to either resistors or collaborators in the face of colonialism. The point I make is that the complexity of the nationalist metanarratives can only be grasped effectively when one transcends the binary categories of the oppressors and the oppressed, the dominator and the dominated, that colonialism itself had imposed. Otherwise any analysis which locks social relations into binary categories is likely to delete the complex engagement with how power was mobilised and contested within Africa. Frantz Fanon hinted at a more multivalent and nuanced approach to African conceptualisation of the people's culture and the general historical movement to which they were giving shape. This complex process, Fanon argued, resided neither in the people's past nor in the basic manichean relations that colonialism had imposed through its racist logic, but in the 'fluctuating movement which they [the people] are just giving shape to, and which, as soon as it has started, will be the signal for everything to be called in question' (Fanon, 1967, p. 183). He adds: 'Let there be no mistake about it; it is to this *zone of occult instability where the people dwell* that we must come; and it is there that our souls are crystallized and that our perceptions and our lives are transfused with light' (p. 183, my emphasis). I think Fanon's split space of 'occult instability' opens up the possibilities of seeing how deeply the colonised subjects were implicated in the modernist project that was engendered by colonialism and how elusive – and difficult to police – the boundary between colonisers and colonised was. It forces us not simply to assert that Africans had history, but rather, to ask how Africans were implicated in establishing or contesting power. Such questions are not easily resolved within the restrictive framework of binarism, even if it may be useful in unlocking power relations in general terms. And to that extent, Ngugi tends to undermine his positive project of restoration and historical contestation due to his recourse to a linear typology of the 'robber and the robbed' that has become the hallmark of his more recent texts.

The implications of Ngugi's historical sense on his charac-terisation are most evident. For example, for Ngugi the native bourgeoisie in Africa is doomed to decadence and parasitism and is therefore incapable of positive and objective self-reflection. Clearly, this is a social deterministic principle built on the speculative axiom that the bourgeoisie is rigid and unable to regenerate itself and the only class capable of providing the true moral guidance is the working class. The oppressors are denied any form of humanity – they are the embodiment of evil – while the oppressed are the embodiment of good. Thus, all negative values are vested with the oppressor class, while all positive values are given to the oppressed. Ngugi's characters serve to illustrate this simple thesis of broad class conflict which he posits as historical subversion and the essence of Kenyan history. What we discern in Ngugi's historical sense are immutable social classes defined once and for all ages. But social classes, as Fredrick Jameson reminds us, are dynamic and diverse in character; it is impossible to imagine a fixed archetype of social types because any social class 'is always characteristic of a given period, of a given decade' (1971, p. 195). Yet Ngugi's Mau Mau fighter in the colonial state (e.g. Kimathi) is not any different from a Mau Mau fighter in the postcolonial state (e.g. Matigari); his revolutionary intellectual and the national bourgeoisie remain the same in all his novels set in entirely different historical moments. By creating the impression that social classes are immutable and fixed for all ages Ngugi again undermines the very dialectics of restoration, that is, historical movement, which is at the heart of his narratives.

However, as I have also attempted to demonstrate in this book, Ngugi is acutely aware of the contradictions inherent in trying to use narrative as a vehicle for illustrating a thesis while attempting to relate the text to the contemporary world. To resolve this contradiction Ngugi has fallen back on the literary modes of didactic narrative. He uses the allegorical mode and a range of popular forms. By returning to the popular forms of his people, Ngugi hopes to transcend his own social and literary reification and to use his art as a tool for political pedagogy. This move is at the heart of his radical shift to write in his indigenous language, Gikuyu. It is, in his words, 'an ever-continuing struggle to seize back creative initiative in history through a real control of all means of communal self-definition in time and space' (Ngugi 1986, p. 4). His use of allegorical typology of characters in which the oppressors are portrayed in grotesque images is a devastating reversal of a manichean class structure, but also a pointer to continuity in change. Whereas in his earlier novels the grotesque image of the body is used to satirise the colonists, in the later novels bodily deformity serves to expose the naked mimicry of Western values and borrowed power of the

African bourgeoisie. It is a pointed satire of those who have turned the postcolony into a theatre stage upon which they enact the absurd dance of death and slavery. And although Ngugi shifts from the more complex allegorical methods in his earlier novels to inflexible ones in the later works, the strategies succeed in transforming his later narratives into national allegories, even if the complexity of their liberating potential may be contested within limits.

Ngugi's problematic, in my view, emanates from his divided desire to steep his narrative in the contemporary world of Kenyan politics – a project which invites a realistic portrayal of society – while at the same time seeking to use the narrative as a mute tool for social transformation – a static form of narrative in which characters are either agents of transformation or repression and stasis. This tension could also be said to be between Ngugi the writer and Ngugi the political activist and mythologiser. In this struggle, especially in his postcolonial narratives, it is Ngugi the activist with his ideological warheads of right and wrong, the oppressed and the oppressor, that triumphs over a deliberate creative imagination that we have tended to associate with Ngugi's earlier narratives.

Notes

Introduction

1. I make exception to Maughan-Brown (1985), *Land, Freedom and Fiction: History and Ideology in Kenya,* which in my view is a pioneering work in the kind of approach I have in mind. Maughan-Brown's otherwise brilliant text is limited to Ngugi's earlier narratives and to Mau Mau historiography. Sichermann (1989) is also a fascinating but limited study of Ngugi and Kenyan historiography.
2. Arthur Marwick (1995) has forcefully challenged White's position. Although Marwick argues correctly that history is not a branch of literature, his casual dismissal of narrative elements in history is hardly convincing. It seems to me that Marwick's otherwise brilliant article is nothing but a return to the empiricist conception of the past – history as 'the study of human past, through the systematic analysis of the primary sources, and the bodies of knowledge arising from that study' (Marwick 1995, p. 12). I take the view here of the past as a discursive construct which does not preclude Marwick's principal methods of retrieving the past, but throws it open as an arena for competing versions of historical recovery. In this sense, the place accorded to literary texts (in relation to other components of the historical record either within the procedures of literary scholarship or within those of historical inquiry), need not be seen as privileging one discipline over the other, but as part of the total project of historical recovery.
3. For me the article has two major problems: first, Glenn's conceptualisation of the 'elite' seems oversimplified and smacks of 'the men of two worlds' approach and second, he tends to see the 'educated elite' as an homogeneous grouping without taking into account the contradictions that exist between various strata of this 'elite'.
4. See for example Tom Nairn (1981); Geoff Eley (1981); J. Sheeban (1981) and Benedict Anderson (1983).
5. Ngugi argues that the colonialist writers like Robert Ruark (1955) and Elspeth Huxley (1961) have tended to give a very

biased account of Kenya's nationalist history, particularly in their portrayal of the Mau Mau war. The suppression of Mau Mau history and the marginalisation of workers and peasants, Ngugi asserts, has also been a major feature of works written by Kenyan historians such as Bethwell A. Ogot (1972), William R. Ochien'g (1972), and Godfrey Muriuki (1974), among others. David Maughan-Brown (1985, pp. 206–29), seems to agree with Ngugi that a definite line of interpretation aimed at discrediting Mau Mau as a nationalist movement was followed by many Kenyan scholars.

6. The subaltern is used here in a double sense. First, it means the dominated and the marginalised groups such as peasants, workers and women in the postcolonial state. Second, it is used also as an analytical category to embrace the colonised subjects, defined solely by their common subordination to the coloniser. In its conception of colonialism, subalternity assumes colonialism's ability to coerce, coopt, and categorise challenges into its own structure of power and ideology. Although not Ngugi's terminology, I use it because it best describes the dyad of resister/oppressor which is central to Ngugi's discourses in Kenya: his tendency to evoke a simple binary opposition between the oppressed and the oppressor, and to isolate it from its context. Thus, the concept of subalternity best sets the limits of Ngugi's discourses on postcolonialism and opens his assumptions to challenge by forcing us to argue 'for the complexity of engagement of Africans with imported institutions and constructs' (Cooper 1994, p. 1534).

7. The radical shift is captured poignantly in his portrayal of the Mau Mau war. In the early novels, including *A Grain of Wheat*, Ngugi gives a more complex picture of the moral dilemma that faced both the loyalists and the fighters during the violent period of the 1950s, while in his postcolonial novels one gets a fairly linear history of the movement in which we have neat camps of the abhorred collaborators on the one hand and the patriotic fighters on the other.

8. For Ngugi's biographical details see Simon Gikandi (1989, pp. 148–56) and David Cook and Michael Okenimpke (1983, pp. 205–8).

9. Ngugi (1993, p. 63) himself acknowledges the centrality of these books in the understanding of African literature.

Chapter 1

1. Mazrui 1972, pp. 17–18, quotes similar attitudes towards ethnicity.

2. According to Fanon, the African revolution has to be powered by the peasants because the African elite has been absorbed in mimicking the culture of the coloniser, while the working class, in Fanon's thinking, has become some kind of labour aristocracy clamouring for the privileges of white workers. It is the peasants and the lumpenproletariat, by contrast, who are the true liberationists. See Fanon (1967, pp. 166–99). A detailed summary of Fanon's theories on the African revolution is to be found in the section dealing with the possible influences on Ngugi's radical shift in the introductory chapter.

3. Ever since the publication of *Homecoming*, in which he declared his support for Mau Mau violence as revolutionary and cleansing, Ngugi has continued to support this position in all his subsequent creative and critical works. In *Barrel of a Pen* he went further to give it a baptismal name, 'Mau Mau Land and Freedom Army', to underscore its revolutionary and libertarian role. In his most recent text, *Moving the Centre*, Ngugi has gone a step further by suggesting that it was 'the Mau Mau armed struggle from 1952 to 1962 which captured the imagination of all East Africa and best symbolized the determination of the African people to be free' (1993, p. 171).

4. Maina wa Kinyatti, who in the past supported the thesis of class consciousness among the Mau Mau fighters, has since changed his position. He writes: 'there was no ideological struggle within the Mau Mau movement to transform nationalist consciousness into class consciousness, nor was there a serious systematic analysis of imperialism, the class struggle, and the relation of socialism to the Kenyan revolutionary process' (1987, p. 131).

5. Bethwell A. Ogot (1972, pp. 134–48) has also dealt with the moral complexity of the Mau Mau.

6. Atieno Odhiambo, in an unpublished paper (1992, pp. 12–15), has also emphasised how the idea of progress was a very important component of African political thought at this time.

7. For Ngugi's elaboration of this binary opposition, see his seminal work (1972, pp. 22–5) and for the more comprehensive treatment see Ngugi 1981, pp. 123–38.

8. Whatever the merits and demerits of the 1992 general elections in Kenya, the results showed a clear pattern of voting on ethnic lines. (See 'Fresh Mandate: President Moi Beats His Opponents in the Race for the Highest Seat in the Land', *The Weekly Review*, Nairobi, 1 January 1993.)

9. The importance of language in defining ethnicity has received attention recently (Hofmeyr 1987, pp. 95–123; Fabian 1983, pp. 165–87).
10. The independent church movements which became the pillar of independent school movements attempted to offer alternatives to missionary education and therefore became major vehicles for political mobilisation among the Gikuyus in the period between 1920 and 1960. Incidentally, Ngugi has tended to suppress the role of independent church movements in Kenya's political struggle, even in works set in the colonial period. For information on the independent school movement see John Anderson (1970, Chapter 8), and Terence Ranger (1965, pp. 56–85).
11. The NCCK is an umbrella body which represents the mainstream protestant churches in Kenya including, among others, the Anglicans.
12. Writers like Leys (in his later work, 1978, 1982); Cowen (1979, 1982a), and Swainson (1980), have cast a great deal of doubt over dependency theories that sought to explain Kenya's underdevelopment purely in terms of a weak periphery solely dependent on a dominant centre. Thus, the theory that the national bourgeoisie is almost nonexistent, and that even the small comprador bourgeoisie that exists works only for and in tandem with the international capital, can no longer hold sway in the face of increasing evidence of the long history of an indigenous bourgeoisie which enjoys the support of the state.

Chapter 2

1. In his prison diary, *Detained*, Ngugi talks of prison conditions as a kind of '[c]olonial Lazarus raised from the dead: this putrid spectre of our recent history haunted us daily at Kamiti prison. It hovered over us, its shadow looming larger and larger in our consciousness as days and nights rolled away without discernible end to our sufferings. We discussed its various shades and aspects, drawing on our personal experiences, often arriving at clashing interpretations and conclusions. Who raised colonial Lazarus from the dead to once again foul the fresh air of Kenya's dawn?' (1981a, p. 63). Evidently, the past was very much a parallel to the present. In the same diary, Ngugi recounts to us the difficulties he faced while writing *Devil on the Cross*, often resorting to using a toilet roll as writing paper (1981a, p. 164).

2. *The Times*, Nairobi, 11 April 1966, as quoted in Odinga (1967, p. 310). See also Ngugi (1981a, p. 89) and his reference to Kenyatta's upbraiding of Kaggia.

Chapter 3

1. See Andrew Scheiber, who contrasts the redundant form of overdetermination with the more complex one, particularly in the realistic novel, which he calls 'semic variegation, in which characters are made more complex through the number and diversity of connotations conferred on them' (1991, p. 265).
2. Of the victim type we have those characters who opposed colonialism or whose parents were involved in the struggle for independence but continue to suffer after independence. These characters go through a stage of disillusionment with independence and ultimately come to the awareness that the struggle has to continue in the postcolonial period. In *Petals of Blood* we have Karega, Abdulla, Wanja, Nyakinyua and Joseph. In *Devil on the Cross*, apart from Wariinga, we also have Wangari and Muturi. In *Matigari* we have Matigari wa Njiruingi, Guthera, Muriuki and worker-leader, Ngaruro wa Kiriro. These are the characters in whom Ngugi invests positive values; characters with whom he sympathises.

Chapter 4

1. In *Decolonising the Mind* Ngugi argues that the African novel has been 'impoverished by the very means of its possible liberation: exposure of its would-be-practitioners to the secular tradition of the critical and socialist realism of the European novel and the entry on the stage of commercial publishers who were outside the colonial government and missionary control' (1986, p. 70).
2. *Devil on the Cross* (1982) and *Matigari* (1987), were first published in Gikuyu and translated into English only much later.
3. For Ngugi's views on the use of popular forms of his people see his chapters on 'The Language of African Theatre' and 'The Language of African Fiction' in *Decolonising the Mind* (1986).
4. One has to admit here that the veracity of Ngugi's claim has not been tested by any independent research into Ngugi's readership. However, statistics from Ngugi's publisher indicate that very few copies of the text were sold and, given

the record of a poor reading culture among Kenya's lower classes, it is unlikely that the book was read by Ngugi's target audience. See Henry Chakava (1993, p. 73).

5. Although mission education in certain cases encouraged the use of local 'folktales' and vernacular in education, this policy was not always pursued consistently. In Kenya, between 1900 and 1940, the British government was hostile to the teaching of English for fear that radical literature might become accessible to Kenyans and emphasis was put on the use of vernacular languages. Significantly, this policy was later changed by Sir Philip Mitchell so that the teaching of English could be a tool for 'establishing British values and standards in Kenya'. Ngugi was a product of this generation, subjected to English literary heritage as 'the Great Tradition'. Recently, Ngugi has written of his alienation: 'Thus language and literature were taking us further and further from ourselves to other selves, from our world to other worlds' (1986, p. 12).

6. See Ngugi 1986, pp. 78–86. In the same text Ngugi also refers to the difficulty that a writer like him is likely to face in trying to satirise what he calls the 'neo-slaves' – the African *petit-bourgeoisie* – 'when their own words beat all fictional exaggerations'. In his view, Moi's 'Nyao' philosophy, in which Moi calls on all Kenyans, particularly his cabinet ministers, to sing like parrots after his tune, 'beat the most satiric genius'.

7. In *Decolonising the Mind* (1986, p. 78), Ngugi acknowledges that he has appropriated certain Christian elements that would help root his works within a known tradition. Evidently Ngugi is also broadening the scope of the popular to incorporate the more recent influences introduced by colonialism, but influences which have impacted on popular discourse among peasants and workers in Kenya.

8. Atieno Odhiambo (1987, pp. 177–201) argues that the 'emergent wisdom was that the strong state was a prerequisite for law, order, good government, and nation-building', but one in which dissent or any form of political discordant was not allowed. He argues that this has been the experience of the postcolonial state in Kenya, leading to a situation where the masses have sought to create their own democratic space – through popular forums such as funerals, *matatu* taxis, football crowds – in which rumour-mongering, 'the highly respected institution ... against which authorities high and low are continually warning', is the most popular vehicle for political discourse.

9. As recently as January 1992, a Kenyan weekly recorded that a strongly worded government statement released by the office of the president condemned the coup rumours and warned that the police were under instructions to take firm action against anyone 'spreading unfounded and malicious rumours whose intention is to cause and spread worry, unrest, fear, despondency and alarm among law-abiding citizens, contrary to Chapter 63, Section 66 (1) and (2) of the Penal Code', *The Weekly Review*, Nairobi, 17 January, 1992, p. 5.

10. According to this survey, Chakava recorded a sales figure of 2,445 in 1986 and a drop in sales to 901 in 1987 for the Gikuyu version of *Matigari*. And for the Gikuyu version of *Devil on the Cross*, he recorded an average sales figure of 334 per year between 1985 and 1987. These figures are extremely low and they can serve only to highlight the ambiguous position that Ngugi's narrative continues to hold, in spite of the writer's recourse to the Gikuyu language and appropriation of popular forms.

Chapter 5

1. Ngugi's image of the prostitute archetype could be contrasted with Buchi Emecheta's attempt to redeem the image of the degraded prostitute and to present it as a viable avenue of escape and liberty for women entrapped within the 'shallow grave' of patriarchy. See, for example, her novel, *The Joys of Motherhood* (London: Heinemann, 1979), in which she gives us a clinical assessment of the plight of women in Nigeria, and demonstrates that the joy of women does not reside in motherhood, and mothering male children for that matter, but rather in rebelling against all forms of patriarchal constraints, even if this entails living by prostitution.

Chapter 6

1. In 'Literature and Society', *Writers In Politics* (Heinemann, 1981, p. 31), where Ngugi laments the absence of positive heroes in African literature, he goes on to show his commitment to socialist transformation when he writes: 'Literature, and our attitudes to literature, can help or else hinder in the creation of a united socialist Black Power in Africa based on the just continuing struggle of peasants and workers for a total control of their productive forces.'

2. Ngugi's idea of 'radical' transformation and resistance is at variance with the less spectacular, less abstract and the more informal forms of resistance which writers like James Scott (1985, pp. 28–47) argue tend to characterise the marginalised groups in society. Scott argues that most subordinate classes throughout history are rarely afforded the luxury of open and organised political activity, but they have continued to express their resistance through forms which are covert, subtle, but effectively subversive.

3. In his last two major works, *Xala* (1976) and *The Last of the Empire* (1983), Ousmane seems to give recognition to the ambivalent nature of the postcolonial state and to draw attention to the fact that the forces of regeneration are never constant, but shifting; that they are multifaceted and spread across class barriers – ranging from street beggars to the reformed patriotic *petit-bougeoisie* as in *Xala*; to the students, the radical journalist, the man of moral force and even to the patriotic army in *The Last of the Empire*. There is a radical shift away from the workers as the only agents of change, therefore, gesturing towards alternative locus of agency within the postcolonial African society.

Bibliography

Works by Ngugi

Weep Not, Child (London: Heinemann, 1964).
The River Between (London: Heinemann, 1965).
A Grain of Wheat (London: Heinemann, 1967).
Homecoming (London: Heinemann, 1972).
'Introduction', Okot P'Bitek, *Africa Cultural Revolution* (Nairobi: EAPH, 1973).
Secret Lives (London: Heinemann, 1975).
with Micere Mugo, *The Trial of Dedan Kimath* (Nairobi: Heinemann, 1976).
Petals of Blood (London: Heinemann, 1977).
'The Changing Image of Women Over the Crucial Historical Phases', *The Participation of Women in Kenya Society*, ed. Achola Pala, Thelma Awori and Abigail Krystal (Nairobi: KLB, 1978).
Interviewed by Amooti wa Irumba, 'The Making of a Rebel', *Index on Censorship*, 9, 3 June (1980) 20–4.
Detained (London: Heinemann, 1981a).
Writers in Politics (London: Heinemann, 1981b).
Devil on the Cross (London: Heinemann, 1982).
Barrel of a Pen (Trenton: African World Press, 1983).
Decolonising the Mind (Nairobi: Heinemann, 1986).
Matigari (London: Heinemann, 1987).
Moving the Centre (Nairobi: East African Educational Publishers, 1993).

Articles and Books

Achebe, Chinua, 'The Novelist as a Teacher', *African Writers on African Writing*, ed. G. D. Killam (London: Heinemann, 1973) 1–4.
Amuka, Peter, 'Oral Reading of the Written: The Example of *Masira ki Ndaki*', Paper given at the Inter-University Workshop on Language and Literature (Eldoret: Moi University, 1993).
Anderson, Benedict, *Imagined Communities: Reflections on the Origin and Spread of Nationalism* (London: Verso, 1983).
Anderson, John, *The Struggle for the School* (London: Longman, 1970).
Armah, Ayi Kwei, *The Beautiful Ones Are Not Yet Born* (London: Heinemann, 1969).
Awonoor, Kofi, *The Breast of the Earth* (New York: NOK, 1976).
Bakhtin, Mikhail M., *Rabelais and His World*, trans. Helene Iswolky (London: MTI Press, 1968).
—, *The Dialogic Imagination: Four Essays*, trans. Caryl Emerson and Michael (Holquist. Austin: University of Texas Press, 1982).

169

Barthes, Roland, *Writing Degree Zero* (New York: Hill and Wang, 1968).
—, *S/Z*, trans. Richard Miller (New York: Hill and Wang 1974).
Bayart, Jean-Francois, *The State in Africa: The Politics of the Belly* (London: Longman, 1993).
Benjamin, Walter, *The Origin of German Tragic Drama* (London: New Left Books, 1977).
Bennet, Tony, *Outside Literature* (London: Routledge, 1990).
Bennet, Tony, Colin Mercer and Janet Wollacott, *Popular Culture and Social Relations* (Milton Keynes: Open University Press, 1986).
Berman, Bruce J. and John Lonsdale, *Unhappy Valley Book One: State and Class* (London: James Currey, 1992a).
—, *Unhappy Valley Book Two: Violence and Ethnicity* (London: James Currey, 1992b).
Brett, E. A., *Colonialism and Underdevelopment in East Africa* (London: Heinemann, 1973).
Buijtenhuijs, R., *Mau Mau Twenty Years After* (The Hague: Mouton, 1973).
Bunyan, J., *Pilgrim's Progress* (London: J. M. Dent, 1954).
Caminero-Santangelo, Byron, 'Neocolonialism and the Betrayal Plot in *A Grain of Wheat*: Ngugi wa Thiong'o's Re-vision of Under Western Eyes', *Research in African Literatures*, 29: 1 (1998) 139–52.
Chakava, Henry, 'A Decade of Publishing in Kenya: 1977–1987. One Man's Involvement', *Reading on Publishing in Africa and the Third World*, ed. P. G. Altbach (New York: Bellagio Publishing, 1993) 67–73.
Chatterjee, Partha, *Nationalist Thought and the Colonial World: A Derivative Discourse* (London: Zed Press, 1986).
—, *The Nation and Its Fragments: Colonial and Postcolonial Histories* (New Jersey: Princeton University Press, 1993).
Clifford, Gay. *The Transformation of Allegory* (London: Routledge & Kegan Paul, 1974).
Clough, Marshall S., *Fighting Two Sides: Kenyan Chiefs and Politicians, 1918-1940* (Niwot: University Press of Colorado, 1990).
Cohen, D. W., 'Position Paper', Fifth International Roundtable in Anthropology and History (Paris: Maison des Sciences de l'Homme, July 1986).
Cook, David and Michael Okenimpke, *Ngugi wa Thiong'o: An Exploration of His Writings* (London: Heinemann, 1983).
Cooper, Brenda, *To Lay These Secrets Open: Evaluating African Writing* (Cape Town: David Phillip Publishers, 1992).
Cooper, Frederick, 'Mau Mau and the Discourses of Decolonization', *Journal of African History*, 29 (1988) 313–20.
—, 'Conflict and Connection: Rethinking Colonial African History', *The American Historical Review*, 99: 5 (1994) 1516–45.
Cowen, M. P., 'Capital and Household Production: The Case of Wattle in Kenya's Central Province, 1903–1964', PhD thesis, Cambridge University, 1979.
—, 'The British State and Agrarian Accumulation in Kenya', *Industry and Accumulation in Africa*, ed. Martin Fransman (London: Heinemann, 1982a) 142–69.
—, 'Some Recent East African Peasant Studies', *Journal of Peasant Studies*, 9: 2 (1982b) 252–61.

—, 'Change in State Power, International Conditions and Peasant Producers: The Case of Kenya', *Journal of Development Studies*, 22: 2 (1986) 355–84.

Davidson, Basil, *Africa in Modern History: The Search for a New Society* (London: Allen Lanes, 1978).

de Man, Paul, *Blindness and Insight: Essays in the Rhetoric of Contemporary Criticism I* (Minneapolis: University of Minnesota Press, 1983).

Desai, G., 'Theatre as Praxis: Discursive Strategies in African Popular Theatre', *African Studies Review*, 33: 1 (1990) 65–92.

Duerden, D. And Pieterse, C. (eds), *African Writers Talking* (London: Heinemann Educational Books, 1972).

Eley, Geoff, 'Nationalism and Social History', *Social History*, 6 (1981) 83–107.

Emecheta, Buchi, *The Joys of Motherhood* (London: Heinemann, 1979).

Fabian, J., 'Missions and the Colonization of African Languages: Developments in the Former Belgian Congo', *Canadian Journal of African Studies*, 17: 2 (1983) 165–87.

Fanon, Frantz, *The Wretched of the Earth*, trans. Constance Farrington (Hamondsworth: Penguin Books, 1967).

Foucault, M. *Language, Counter Memory, Practice* (New York: Cornell University Press, 1984).

Furedi, Frank, *The Mau Mau War in Perspective* (London: James Currey, 1989).

Gecau, R. N., *Kikuyu Folktales: Their Nature and Value* (Nairobi: KLB, 1976).

Gertzel, C. J., M. Goldschmidt and D. Rothchild, *Government and Politics in Kenya* (Nairobi: EAEP, 1969).

Gikandi, S., 'The Growth of the East African Novel', *The Writing of East and Central Africa*, ed. G. D. Killam (London: Heinemann, 1984) 231–46.

—, *Reading the African Novel* (Nairobi: Heinemann, 1987).

—, 'On Culture and the State: The Writings of Ngugi wa Thiong'o', *Research in African Literatures*, 22: 4 (1989) 148–56.

—, 'The Epistemology of Translation: Ngugi, Matigari and the Politics of Language', *Research in African Literatures*, 22: 4 (1991) 161–7.

—, 'Ngugi's Conversion: Writing and the Politics of Language', *Research in African Literatures*, 23: 1 (1992) 131–44.

Glenn, Ian, 'Ngugi wa Thiong'o and the Dilemma of the Intellectual Elite in Africa: A Sociological Perspective', *English in Africa*, 8: 2 (1981) 53–66.

Gramsci, Antonio, *Selections from Prison Note Books* (New York: International Publishers, 1978).

Gurnah, Abdulrazak, 'Matigari: A Tract of Resistance', *Research in African Literatures*, 22: 4 (1991) 169–72.

—, 'Transformative Strategies in the Fiction of Ngugi wa Thiong'o', *Essays on African Writing: A Re-evaluation*, ed. A. Gurnah (London: Heinemann, 1993) 142–58.

Hall, Stuart, David Held and Tony McGrew (eds), *Modernity and its Features* (Cambridge: Polity Press, 1992).

Haugerud, Angelique, *The Culture of Politics in Modern Kenya* (London: Cambridge University Press, 1995).

Hofmeyr, Isabel, 'Building a Nation From Words: Afrikaans Language, Literature and Ethnic Identity, 1902–1924', *The Politics of Race, Class and Nationalism in Twentieth-Century South Africa*, ed. Shula Marks and Stanley Trapido (London: Longman, 1987) 95–123.

Huxley, Elspeth, *A Thing to Love* (London: Chatto & Windus, 1961).

Jameson, Fredrick, *Marxism and Form* (Princeton: Methuen, 1971).

—, 'Reflection in Conclusion', *Aesthetics and Politics* (London: New Left Books, 1977).

—, *The Political Unconscious: Narrative as a Socially Symbolic Act* (New York: Cornell University Press, 1982).

—, 'Third World Literature in the Era of Multinational Capitalism', *Pretexts*, 3 (1991) 82–104.

JanMohamed, Abdul R., *Manichean Aesthetics: The Politics of Literature in Colonial Africa* (Amherst: University of Massachusetts Press, 1983).

Julien, Eileen, *African Novels and the Question of Orality* (Bloomington: Indiana University Press, 1992).

Kabira, W. Mukabi and Karega wa Mutahi, *Gikuyu Oral Literature* (Nairobi: Heinemann, 1988).

Kabiro, N., *Man in the Middle* (Richmond, B.C.: L.S.M. Press, 1973).

Kanogo, M. J. Thabitha, *Squatters and the Roots of Mau Mau 1905–63* (London: Heinemann, 1987).

Kenyatta, Jomo, *Suffering Without Bitterness* (Nairobi: EAPH, 1968).

—, *Facing Mount Kenya* (London: Heinemann, 1979).

Kgositsile, W. Keorapetse, 'Towards Our Theatre: A Definitive Act', *Black Expression* (New York: Weybright, 1969) 145–9.

Killam, G. D. (ed.), *Critical Perspectives on Ngugi wa Thiong'o* (Washington, DC: Three Continents, 1984).

Kilson, Martin L., 'Land and the Kikuyu: A Study of the Relationship Between Land and Kikuyu Political Movements', *Journal of Negro History*, 2 (1955) 103–53.

Kinyatti, Maina wa, 'Mau Mau: The Peak of African Nationalism in Kenya', *Kenya Historical Review*, 5: 2 (1977) 287–391.

—, *Thunder from the Mountains: Mau Mau Patriotic Songs* (London: Zed Press, 1980).

—, (ed.), *Kenya's Freedom Struggle: The Dedan Kimathi Papers* (London: Zed Press, 1987).

Kitching, Gavin, *Class and Economic Change in Kenya: The Making of an African Petite Bourgeoisie* (New Haven: Yale University Press, 1980).

Kunene, Daniel, *Thomas Mofolo and the Emergence of Written Sesotho Prose* (Johannesburg: Ravan Press, 1989).

Langdon, Steven, 'Multinational Corporations, Taste, Transfer, and Underdevelopment: A Case Study from Kenya', *Review of African Political Economy*, 2 (1975) 12–35.

—, 'The State and Capitalism in Kenya', *African Political Economy Review*, 8 (1977) 90–8.

—, *Multinational Corporations in the Political Economy of Kenya* (London: Macmillan, 1981).

Lazarus, Neil, *Resistance in Postcolonial African Fiction* (New Haven: Yale University Press, 1992).

—, 'Disavowing Decolonization: Fanon, Nationalism, and the Problematic of Representation in Current Theories of Colonial Discourse', *Research in African Literatures*, 24: 4 (1993) 69–98.

Lenin, V. I., 'Imperialism, the Highest Stage of Capitalism', *Lenin: Selected Works* (Moscow: Progress Publishers, 1968) 169–257.

Leys, Colin, *Underdevelopment in Kenya: The Political Economy of Neo-colonialism 1964–1971* (London: Heinemann, 1974).

—, 'Capital Accumulation, Class Formation and Dependency: The Significance of the Kenyan Case.', *Socialist Register*. eds. Ralph Miliband and John Savole (London: Martin Press, 1978) 241–66.

—, 'Kenya: What Does "Dependency" Explain?' *Review of African Political Economy*, 17 (1980) 109–13.

—, 'Accumulation, Class Formation and Dependency: Kenya', *Industry and Accumulation in Africa*, ed. Martin Fransman (London: Heinemann, 1982) 170–92.

Lindfors, B., 'Ngugi wa Thiong'o's Early Journalism', *World Literature Written in English*, 20 (1981) 23–41.

Lo Liyong, Taban, *The Last Word* (Nairobi: EAEP, 1969).

Maloba, O. Wunyabari, *Mau Mau and Kenya: An Analysis of a Peasant Revolt* (Bloomington: Indiana University Press, 1993).

Mare, Gerhard, *Brothers Born of Warrior Blood: Politics and Ethnicity in South Africa* (Johannesburg: Ravan Press, 1992).

Marwick, Arthur, 'Two Approaches to Historical Study: The Metaphysical (Including "Postmodernism") and the Historical', *Journal of Contemporary History*, 30 (1995) 5–34.

Maughan-Brown, David, *Land, Freedom and Fiction: History and Ideology in Kenya* (London: Zed Press, 1985).

Mazrui, Ali, *Cultural Engineering and Nation Building in East Africa* (Illinois: North Western University Press, 1972).

—, *Nationalism and New States in Africa from about 1935 to the Present* (Nairobi: Heinemann, 1984).

Mbembe, Achille, 'Provisional Notes on the Postcolony', *Africa*, 62: 1 (1992) 3–35.

Mink, Louis O., 'Narrative Form as a Cognitive Instrument', *The Writing of History and Historical Understanding*, ed. Robert H. Canary and Henry Kozucku (Madison: University of Wisconsin Press, 1978) 132–49.

Mudimbe, V. Y., *The Invention of Africa: Gnosis, Philosophy, and Order of Knowledge* (Bloomington: Indiana University Press, 1988).

Mudrick, Marvin, 'Character and Event in Fiction', *Yale Review*, 50 (Winter 1961) 202–18.

Mugo, Micere, *African Women*, 6, Sept–Oct (1976) 14–15.

—, 'The Role of Women in the Struggle for Freedom', *The Participation of Women in Kenya Society* Achola Pala, Thelma Awori and Abigail Krystal (London: KLB, 1978) 210–19.

Muriuki, Godfrey, *A History of the Kikuyu,1500–1900* (Nairobi: Oxford University Press, 1974).

Nairn, Tom, 'The Modern Janus', *The Break Up of Britain* (London: Oxford University Press, 1981).

Ndebele, Njabulo S., *Rediscovery of the Ordinary: Essays on South African Literature and Culture* (Johannesburg: COSAW, 1991).

Ndigirigi, Gichingiri, 'Character Names and Types in Ngugi's *Devil on the Cross'*, *UFAHAMU*, XIX, II & III, (1991) 96–109.

Ngara, Emmanuel, *Art and Ideology in the African Novel: A Study on the Influence of Marxism on African Writing* (London: Heinemann, 1985).

Nkosi, Lewis, *Tasks and Masks* (London: Longman, 1981).

Nkrumah, Kwame, *Neo-Colonialism: The Last Stage of Imperialism* (London: Heinemann, 1968).

Nyangira, N., 'Ethnicity, Class and Politics in Kenya', *The Political Economy of Kenya*, ed. Michael Schatzberg (New York: Praeger Publisher, 1987) 15–32.

Ochien'g William R., 'Colonial African Chiefs – Were They Primarily Self-Seeking Scoundrels?' *Politics and Nationalism in Colonial Kenya*, ed. B.A. Ogot (Nairobi: EAPH, 1972) 46–70.

Odhiambo, E. S. Atieno, *The Paradox of Collaboration and Other Essays* (Nairobi: EALB, 1974).

—, 'Democracy and the Ideology of Order in Kenya' in Schatzberg (1987), 177–201.

—, 'The Production of History in Kenya: The Mau Mau Debate', *Canadian Journal of African Studies*, 25: 2 (1991) 300–7.

—, 'The Tyranny of Property and Models of the Future: Towards Mau Mau in Kenya, 1945–1955', Paper presented to Program on Agrarian Studies, Yale University, 14 Feb. 1992.

Odinga, Oginga, *Not Yet Uhuru* (London: Heinemann, 1967).

—, *Oginga, Odinga: His Philosophy and Beliefs*, introduction by Odera H. Oruka (Nairobi: Initiatives Publishers, 1992).

Ogot, Bethwell. A., 'Revolt of the Elders', *Politics and Nationalism in Kenya* ed. B.A. Ogot (Nairobi: EAPH, 1972) 134–48.

Ousmane, Sembene, *God's Bits of Wood* (London: Heinemann, 1970).

—, *Xala* (London: Heinemann, 1976).

—, *The Last of the Empire* (London: Heinemann, 1983).

Piper, Laurence, Sihle Shange and Volker Wedekind, 'Ethnicity and Contest Over Meaning: Considerations on Ethnicity Based on a Case Study of School-going Youth in the Greater Pietermaritzburg Area', Unpublished Paper: University of Natal, 1992.

Ranger, Terence, 'African Attempts to Control Education in East and Central Africa, 1900–1939', *Past and Present*, 32 (1965) 56–85.

—, 'Connexions Between "Primary Resistance" Movements and Modern Mass Nationalism in East Africa, Part 1', *Journal of African History*, 9: 3 (1968) 437–8.

—, 'Missionaries, Migrants and the Manyika: The Invention of Ethnicity in Zimbabwe', *The Creation of Tribalism in Southern Africa*, ed. Leroy Vail (London: James Currey, 1989) 118–49.

Robson, C.B., *Ngugi wa Thiong'o* (New York: Macmillan, 1975).

Rodney, Walter, *How Europe Underdeveloped Africa* (Dar-es-Salaam: Tanzania Publishing House, 1976).

Roseberg, G. Carl and John Nottingham. *The Myth of Mau Mau: Nationalism in Kenya* (London: Oxford University Press, 1966).

Ruark, Robert, *Something of Value* (London: Hamish Hamilton, 1955).

Said, Edward, 'Reflections on Exile', *Granta*, 13 (Autumn 1984) 158–65.

—, *Culture and Imperialism* (London: Vintage, 1994).

Schatzberg, Michael G. (ed.), *The Political Economy of Kenya* (New York: Praeger Publishers, 1987).

Scheiber, Andrew J., 'Sign, Seme, and the Psychological Character: Some Thoughts on Roland Barthes' *S/Z* and the Realistic Novel', *The Journal of Narrative Technique*, 21: 3 (Fall 1991) 262–73.

Scholes, Robert and Robert Kellog, *The Nature of Narrative* (New York: Oxford University Press, 1966).

Scott, J. C., *Weapons of the Weak* (New Haven: Yale University Press, 1985).

Sheeban, J., 'What Is German History? Reflections on the Role of the Nation in German History and Historiography', *Journal of Modern History*, 53 (1981) 1–23.

Shreve, Anita, 'Interview with Ngugi', *Viva Magazine*, Nairobi (July 1977).

Sichemann, Carol M., 'Ngugi wa Thiong'o and the Writing of Kenyan History', *Research in African Literature*, 20: 3 (1989) 347–70.

Slemon, Stephen, 'Monuments of Empire: Allegory/Counter-Discourse/Post-Colonial Writing', *Kunapipi*, 9: 3 (1987) 1–34.

—, 'Post-Colonial Allegory and the Transformation of History', *Journal of Commonwealth Literature*, 32: 1 (1988) 157–81.

Smith, Craig V., 'The Stereography of Class, Race, and Nation in *God's Bits of Wood*', *Research in African Literatures*, 24: 1 (1993) 51–66.

Sommer, Doris, 'Allegory and Dialectics: A Match Made in Romance', *boundary* 2, 18: 1 (Spring 1991) 60–82.

Stratton, Florence, *Contemporary African Literature and the Politics of Gender* (London: Routledge, 1994).

Swainson, N., *The Development of Corporate Capitalism in Kenya* (London: Heinemann, 1980).

Tarmakin, M., 'Mau Mau in Nakuru', *Journal of African History*, 17: 1 (1976) 24–32.

—, 'The Loyalists in Nakuru During the Mau Mau Revolt and its Aftermath, 1953–1963', *Asian and African Studies*, 12: 2 (1978) 247–61.

Vail, Leroy (ed.), *The Creation of Tribalism in Southern Africa* (London: James Currey, 1989).

White, Hayden, *The Content of the Form: Narrative Discourse and Historical Representation* (Baltimore: Johns Hopkins University Press, 1987).

White, Luise, *The Comforts of Home: Prostitution in Colonial Nairobi* (Chicago: University of Chicago Press, 1990).

Newspapers and Magazines

The Weekly Review, Nairobi, 30 March 1984.
The Weekly Review, Nairobi, 17 January 1992.
The Weekly Review, Nairobi, 19 June 1992.
The Weekly Review, Nairobi, 24 July 1992.

Index

Index by Sue Carlton